slated.
osts

...uxe Books) and *The Loving-Cup* (... ...iscat
edited *100 Favourite Scottish Poems* (Scottish Poetry
...uath Press), and has also published plays and a memoir,
s (Scottish Cultural Press). He has received awards from
...ottish Arts Council, Society of Authors and Poetry Book
...ety am...ng others. Born in Glasgow, he grew up in Ayrshire and
...s lived in Edinburgh for many years. From 2002 to 2005 he was
the capital's first official poet laureate.

D0993482

...00024

Also in the '*100 Favourite Poems*' series

100
FAVOURITE
SCOTTISH
LOVE
POEMS

EDITED BY STEWART CONN

Luath Press Limited
EDINBURGH
www.luath.co.uk

**Essex County
Council Libraries**

First published 2008

ISBN (10): 1-906307-66-0
ISBN (13): 978-1-906307-66-0

Selection, introduction and notes © Stewart Conn
Acknowledgements of permission to reprint copyright material are set
out on the pages following the dedication and constitute an extension of
the copyright page. All rights reserved.

The publishers acknowledge the support of

 Scottish
Arts Council

towards the publication of this volume.

The paper used in this book is neutral sized and recyclable. It is made
from elemental chlorine free pulps sourced from renewable forests.

Printed in the UK by
CPI Bookmarque, Croydon CRO 4TD.

Typeset in ITC Charter and Gill Sans by
3btype.com

For Judy

Light hurtling at 186,000 miles
per second, what the eye sees
of that comet and its gas-trail
on its giddy jaunt through space
takes 12 minutes to reach us.

The power of lenses and mirrors
wondrous as ever. Even more
of a marvel, the way the brightness
in your eyes travels towards me
at the implausible speed of love.

ACKNOWLEDGEMENTS

Our thanks are due to the following authors, publishers and estates who have generously given permission to reproduce poems:

Marion Angus, 'Heart-free' from *Voices from their Ain Countrie: The Poems of Marion Angus and Violet Jacob* (ASLS, 2006), reproduced courtesy of Alan J. Byatt; J. K. Annand, 'Aa My Thochts' from *Selected Poems 1925–1990* (Mercat Press, 1992), reproduced courtesy of Scottish Language Dictionaries; Meg Bateman, 'Dòmhnall nan Dòmhnall' reproduced courtesy of the author and 'Fhir luraich 's fhir àlain/Oh bonnie man, lovely man' from *Selected Poems* (Polygon, 1997), reproduced courtesy of Polygon, an imprint of Birlinn Ltd, www.birlinn.co.uk; Pamela Beasant, 'Out with my Loves on a Windy Day' reprinted with permission from *Running with a Snow Leopard* (Two Ravens Press, 2008); Stan Bell, 'Banner Bright' from *In Search of Stansylvania* (Schiltron, 2006), reproduced courtesy of Schiltron; Eleanor Brown, 'Bitcherel' from *Maiden Speech* (Bloodaxe Books, 1996), reproduced courtesy of Bloodaxe Books; George Bruce, 'Sonnet on my wife's birthday' from *Today Tomorrow: The Collected Poems of George Bruce 1933–2000* (Polygon, 2001), reproduced courtesy of Polygon, an imprint of Birlinn Ltd, www.birlinn.co.uk; Tom Buchan, 'The Loch Ness Monster' reproduced courtesy of Lawrence Buchan; Elizabeth Burns, 'The Secret' from *The Lantern Bearers* (Shoestring Press, 2007), reproduced courtesy of John Lucas; John Burnside, 'Husbandry' from *Selected Poems* (Jonathan Cape, 2006), reprinted by permission of The Random House Group Ltd; Ron Butlin, 'The Lake at Preda' from *Without a Backward Glance: New and Selected Poems* (Barzan Publishing, 2005), reproduced courtesy of the author; Gerry Cambridge, 'Ditty' from *Madame Fi-Fi's Farewell and Other Poems* (Luath Press, 2003), reproduced courtesy of Luath Press Ltd; Ken Cockburn, 'Polytheron' from *On the Flyleaf* (Luath Press, 2007), reproduced courtesy of Luath Press Ltd; Stewart Conn, 'Night Sky' (dedicatory poem) from *Stolen Light: Selected Poems* (Bloodaxe Books, 1999) reprinted courtesy of Bloodaxe Books; Joe Corrie, 'The Lover' reproduced courtesy of Morag Corrie; Robert Crawford, 'The Tip of My Tongue' from *Selected Poems* (Chatto and Windus, 2005), reprinted by permission of The Random House Group Ltd; Iain Crichton Smith, 'The Shadows' and 'Shores' from *Collected Poems* (Carcanet, 1992), reproduced courtesy of Carcanet Press Ltd; Anna Crowe, 'Scops Owl' from *Punk with Dulcimer* (Peterloo Poets, 2005), reproduced courtesy of Peterloo Poets; Helen Cruickshank, 'Shy Geordie' reproduced courtesy of Flora Hunter; Des Dillon, 'Sex Education' from *Picking Brambles and other poems* (Luath Press, 2003), reproduced courtesy of Luath Press Ltd; Carol Ann Duffy, 'Finding the Words' from *Rapture* (Picador, 2005), reproduced courtesy of Pan MacMillan; Douglas Dunn, 'France' from *New Selected Poems 1964–2000* (Faber, 2003), reproduced courtesy of Faber &

Faber Ltd; G. F. Dutton, 'Fracture' from *The Bare Abundance: Selected Poems 1975–2001* (Bloodaxe Books, 2002), reproduced courtesy of Bloodaxe Books; Magi Gibson, 'Just Like Eve' from *Wild Women of a Certain Age* (Chapman, 2000), reproduced courtesy of Joy Hendry; Valerie Gillies, 'Glen Isla Love Song' from *Love for Love* (Pocketbooks, 2000), reproduced courtesy of the author; John Glenday, 'Landscape with Flying Man' from *Love for Love* (Pocketbooks, 2000), reproduced courtesy of the author; Sydney Goodsir Smith, 'My Luve, my Luve' reproduced courtesy of Calder Publications; Rody Gorman, 'Love' reproduced courtesy of the author; W. S. Graham, 'I leave this at your ear' from *New Collected Poems* (Faber, 2004), reproduced courtesy of Michael and Margaret Snow; Alexander Gray, 'The Cautious Lover' reproduced with permission of daughter Alison Webster; Andrew Greig, 'A Long Shot' from *This Life, This Life: New & Selected Poems* (Bloodaxe Books, 2006), reproduced courtesy of Bloodaxe Books; George Gunn, 'In Thurso one night' from *Winter Barley* (Chapman, 2005), reproduced courtesy of Joy Hendry; Ian Hamilton Finlay, 'Mansie considers Peedie Mary' from 'Orkney Lyrics' in *The Dancers Inherit the Party: Early Stories, Plays and Poems* (Polygon, 2004), reproduced courtesy of Polygon, an imprint of Birlinn Ltd, www.birlinn.co.uk; Hamish Henderson, 'Vivamus Mea Lesbia Atque Amemus' reproduced courtesy of Felicity Henderson; Diana Hendry, 'Why it Took so Long' from *Heart to Risk* (Uneven Press, 2008), reproduced courtesy of the author; Violet Jacob, 'Tam i' the Kirk', from *Voices from their Ain Countrie: The Poems of Marion Angus and Violet Jacob* (ASLS, 2006), reproduced courtesy of Malcolm Hutton; Kathleen Jamie, 'Suitcases' from *Jizzen* (Picador, 1999) reproduced courtesy of Pan MacMillan; Jackie Kay, 'The Red Graveyard' from *Darling: New & Selected Poems* (Bloodaxe Books, 2007), reproduced courtesy of Bloodaxe Books; Tom Leonard, 'Storm Damage' reproduced courtesy of the author; Liz Lochhead, 'A Night In' from *The Colour of Black & White* (Polygon, 2003), reproduced courtesy of Polygon, an imprint of Birlinn Ltd, www.birlinn.co.uk; Roddy Lumsden, 'Yeah Yeah Yeah' from *Mischief Night: New & Selected Poems* (Bloodaxe Books, 2004), reproduced courtesy of Bloodaxe Books; Norman MacCaig, 'Incident' from *The Poems of Norman MacCaig* (Polygon, 2003), reproduced courtesy of Polygon, an imprint of Birlinn Ltd, www.birlinn.co.uk; Hugh MacDiarmid, 'Wheesht, Wheesht' from *Complete Poems, Vol 1* (Carcanet, 2000), reproduced courtesy of Carcanet Press Ltd; George Mackay Brown, 'Country Girl' from *Collected Poems* (John Murray, 2005), reproduced courtesy of Archie Bevan; Sorley MacLean, 'Traighean' from *From Wood to Ridge* (Carcanet, 1999), reproduced courtesy of Carcanet Press Ltd; Anne MacLeod, 'There will be no end', reproduced courtesy of the author; Aonghas MacNeacail, 'òran luaidh/lovesong/waulking song' reproduced courtesy of the author; Brian McCabe, 'Other Life' from *Body Parts* (Canongate, 1999), reproduced courtesy of Canongate Books; Robert McLellan, 'Sang' reproduced courtesy of John McLellan; Angela McSeveney,

'Bouquet' from *Coming Out With It* (Polygon, 1992), reproduced courtesy of the author; John C. Milne, 'Proposal' reproduced courtesy of Margaret Duncan; William Montgomerie, 'Saint Valentine's Day' reproduced courtesy of Dian Montgomerie Elvin, representing the Montgomerie Literary Estate; Edwin Morgan, 'One Cigarette' from *Collected Poems* (Carcanet, 1996), reproduced courtesy of Carcanet Press Ltd; Edwin Muir, 'Love's Remorse' from *Collected Poems* (Faber, 1960), reproduced courtesy of Faber & Faber; Donald Murray, 'Love-making in St Kilda' reproduced courtesy of the author; William Neill, 'First Love' from *Selected Poems 1969–92* (Canongate, 1994), reproduced courtesy of Canongate Books; Helena Nelson, 'Falling in love' from *Unsuitable Poems* (HappenStance, 2005), reproduced courtesy of the author; Liz Niven, 'Walking Glen Trool' from *Burning Whins* (Luath Press, 2004), reproduced courtesy of Luath Press Ltd; Don Paterson, 'The Thread' from *Landing Light* (Faber, 2003), reproduced courtesy of Faber & Faber; Tom Pow, 'Island Love' reproduced courtesy of the author; John Purser, 'Amoretti XIII' reproduced courtesy of the author; Alastair Reid, 'For Her Sake' reproduced courtesy of the author; Alan Riach, 'Of Love' from *Clearances* (Scottish Cultural Press, 2001), reproduced courtesy of Scottish Cultural Press; James Robertson, 'Love' and 'Sonnet (My love grows)' reproduced courtesy of the author; Robin Robertson, 'To my Daughters, Asleep' from *Swithering* (Picador, 2006), reproduced courtesy of Pan MacMillan; William Soutar, 'Ballad (O! Surely ye hae seen my luve...)' reproduced courtesy of The Trustees of the National Library of Scotland; Sheila Templeton, 'Hot Chick' reproduced courtesy of the author; Derick Thomson, 'Chaill mi mo chridhe riut/I lost my heart to you' reproduced courtesy of the author; Gael Turnbull, 'Your Hands, Their Touch', reproduced courtesy of Jill Turnbull, literary executor; Hamish Whyte, 'Between' from *A Bird in the Hand* (Shoestring Press, 2008), reproduced courtesy of the author; Douglas Young, 'Luve' reproduced courtesy of Clara Young.

Every effort has been made to trace the copyright holders of poems published in this book. If any material has been included without the appropriate acknowledgement, the publishers would be glad to correct this in future editions.

CONTENTS

Acknowledgements

Introduction

Notes

Index of Poets

INTRODUCTION

Just as love and loss are the great themes of song, so there must be more poems about love, its rapture and sorrow, than on any other subject. Scottish poetry is no exception. Indeed the preface to *English Love Poems*, edited by John Betjeman and Geoffrey Taylor, concedes: 'The greatest love poet in these islands was, we think, Robert Burns, but his best love poems are almost always in Scottish dialect and if we were to admit Scottish dialect poems and beautiful Irish love poems ... this anthology would have been twice its size'. Certainly the sheer abundance of riches at my disposal made editing this book both a challenge and a delight.

When *100 Favourite Scottish Poems* came out in 2006 one reviewer asked, 'Whose favourites are they?' I was able to point out that a score of pieces, among them Burns's rousing 'A Man's a Man', had formed the shortlist for a BBC Radio Scotland listeners' poll. There followed a library trawl while I sounded, some might say pestered, fellow poets and readers with a view to presenting as broad a spectrum as possible, without turning somersaults – the acid test for each poem being to read it aloud. Finally, from my own cascading shelves, I sifted more recent work I felt would please.

This time round the responsibility rests solely on my shoulders. As before I scoured other anthologies for work of proven appeal, but without slavishly mimicking them: there can come a stage when even an old favourite, like an old horse, has to be put out to grass. That's to say I followed my nose, but not ignoring the past. 'Bonny Barbara Allan', the radiance of love's dawning from 'The Kingis Quair' and Mark Alexander Boyd's 'Cupid and Venus' rub shoulders with the comic grotesquery of Francis Sempill's 'Blythesome Bridal', Sir Walter Scott's jaunty 'Jock o' Hazeldean' and a snippet from James Hogg.

Andrew Lang from Selkirk and Robert McLellan, who lived on Arran but was of Lanarkshire farm stock, doff their hats to poets from the Central Belt, Buchan, the Western Isles, Orkney and Shetland. That's to say, frae a' the airts. 'A Rondel of Luve' by the 16th century makar Alexander Scott, and a conceit by his 20th century Aberdonian namesake, are countered by the localised dialects of Violet Jacob and John C. Milne. Circling the dance-floor are MacCaig and MacDiarmid, Morgan and Mackay Brown, Douglas Dunn, Tom Leonard, Liz Lochhead, Carol Ann Duffy and Jackie Kay. With them appear (an opportunity too good to miss) often less well-known poems which further reflect the vibrancy of Scottish poetry today and will, I hope, also establish themselves as favourites.

The sole Gaelic contribution to the earlier volume was Sorley MacLean's 'Hallaig', from the BBC shortlist. Not speaking the tongue I didn't feel entitled to pass judgement on other poetry in Gaelic. This time and given the theme, I felt bound to reflect its distinctive flavour. Contributions range from a section of Sorley MacLean's 'Dàin do Eimhir' translated by Iain Crichton Smith to a rendering by Valerie Gillies of a Glen Isla love song.

Spanning 16 centuries are other translations (a mode very much part of our literary heritage) from Latin, French and German. Each adopts an appropriate verse form, and is garbed in a distinctive brand of Scots. As throughout, my final yardstick has been personal preference, and gut feeling.

Previous anthologists tended to group things thematically (First Love, Marriage, Farewells...). I preferred a seamless format, so that pieces in differing moods can raise an eyebrow across the page. It seemed only proper to avoid any overlap with either *100 Favourite Scottish Poems* or (Burns aside) *100 Favourite Scottish Poems to Read Out Loud*, edited by Gordon Jarvie. This ruled out poems by Marion Angus and William Soutar in the former, Edwin Muir and Don Paterson in the latter. I hope I've provided attractive alternatives – likewise there is a short piece from the days when the love-sick young Robert Louis Stevenson was observed skating 'like a melancholy minnow' on Duddingston Loch. But no replacement could be conjured for William Dunbar's address 'to his Ladye' or the Marquis of Montrose 'to his Mistress', both in my own first volume.

In contrast to the courtly elegance and metaphysical wit of so much early English love poetry, a recurring Scottish hallmark is its down-to-earth directness. Prevalent, too (think of the ballads), is the supernatural. The conjunction of these is nowhere more memorable (or macabre) than in 'Clerk Saunders', the murdered knight reappearing not as a disembodied ghost but as an incarnate creature his grief-stricken lover dare not kiss.

A convention familiar in Gaelic poetry is to identify the loved-one with an object in nature. One of the praise-poems here reverses the prevalent image of man and woman as 'hunter and hunted', with a Swan giving chase to a Fox, not the other way round.

Ahead, then, lie romantic fancy and desire, tenderness in age, the poignancy of loneliness and loss, being between loves, and a yearning for love itself, alongside touching glimpses of parental and familial affection. Ringing the changes are sporadic whiffs of love spurned, sour grapes and reminders that at times 'scarting and biting is the Scots folks' wooing'.

In a literary context, of course, any emotional outpouring must be governed and measured, its flame tempered by technique. Many great songs would be poor poems. Rather than risk opening the floodgates, I've disregarded these. Not that love songs are absent (look no further than the verbal melody of Burns); but I hope those included work as poems. Nor does this preclude musicality. On the contrary I suspect this quality more than any other realises the emotional register of a love poem, rendering it memorable not least to its recipient.

Lovers often share an awareness, and a heightened perception, of their surroundings. Here is a kaleidoscopic Scotland of rural and urban settings, past and present, of cliff-top and island scenes, flora and fauna, barley-fields and shorelines, the caprices of weather, even the Loch Ness Monster.

Many of the poems convey a joy shared. Hand in hand with this the qualities by which I hope the selection is most imbued are passion and compassion, warmth and humanity. These so permeate Burns's lyrics that I felt he had to be the one poet with more than a single contribution (five in all).

Their occasions and recipients range from cavorting 'amang the rigs wi' Annie' and rhapsodies of marital and extra-marital bliss, to anguish and despair at love unrequited or lost. What are so striking, when he sheds the swagger of 'Rab Mossgiel' and ignores the urgings of the Edinburgh *literati,* are the directness and tenderness, often bitter-sweetness, of their vernacular – and their crystal clarity. For someone his schoolmaster called 'untunable' he had an ear like an angel.

Was he more in thrall to the lassies or to the deed itself? 'One early song', he asserted, 'was, at the time, real': but in the act of partaking or the moment of composing? He said, 'When I sing of Miss Davies or Miss Lesley Baillie, I have only to feign the passion – the charms are real'. Nothing so trite as infatuation, but always *passion*, demanding all or nothing, possessing him and to which he surrendered, expecting others to follow suit.

What ultimately pierces the heart is his tremulous evocation of human transience. Take the hyperbolic pledge of eternal devotion in 'A Red, Red Rose'; the magical moment in 'Mary Morison' 'when to the trembling string, / The dance gaed through the lighted ha'; or again the poignant role-reversal of 'O, Wert Thou in the Cauld Blast', written for Jessie Lewars, the 17-year-old tending him in his last illness. Only now it isn't just love or a love object, real or fanciful, that is slipping away, but life itself.

In my schooldays you could be belted for not learning Burns by heart (an ironic use of the term) or for using in class Scots words licensed only in the poems. Other than that poetry was considered an effete activity. The poets we were taught belonged exclusively to the Dead Poets' Society, and an English one at that. There has since been a sea-change. Not just reading but writing it are nowadays as natural as breathing. Indeed the latter at times seems to have outrun the former, such the spread of workshops, creative writing groups, self-publishing courses and competitions of all shapes and sizes.

Consistent with this there is a much wider acceptance that besides being educational in the narrow sense, poetry can operate at many levels, whether in giving entertainment or providing solace, inducing simultaneous laughter and tears, or sharpening our perceptions and stimulating memory. It can also illumine our lives.

To do so a poem must speak not merely for the poet but to the reader, and give expression to the latter's intimate feelings – which is why people in love turn to poetry. I hope different poems here will strike a chord with different readers, and ideally the same reader at different times, in varying moods; and that they will provide both a touchstone and a mirror in which the reader (or hearer) can be revealed as the lover... or loved-one. What they have in common is, after all, the language of the heart.

My thanks are due to Gavin MacDougall of Luath who having mooted a possible follow-up to *100 Favourite Scottish Poems*, took the idea for this volume on board, and to Leila Cruickshank for her enthusiastic assistance; to Lizzie MacGregor of the Scottish Poetry Library for readily-proffered guidance; and to the poets themselves for the pleasure I trust their work will give.

Stewart Conn,
August, 2008

1

LOVE'S LIKE A DIZZINESS

James Hogg 1770–1835

O! love! love! laddie,
Love's like a dizziness!
It winna let a puir body
Gang about his business!

2

ONE CIGARETTE

Edwin Morgan b. 1920

No smoke without you, my fire.
After you left,
your cigarette glowed on in my ashtray
and sent up a long thread of such quiet grey
I smiled to wonder who would believe its signal
of so much love. One cigarette
in the non-smoker's tray.
As the last spire
trembles up, a sudden draught
blows it winding into my face.
Is it smell, is it taste?
You are here again, and I am drunk on your tobacco lips.
Out with the light.
Let the smoke lie back in the dark.
Till I hear the very ash
sigh down among the flowers of brass
I'll breathe, and long past midnight, your last kiss.

3

MARY MORISON

Robert Burns 1759–96

O Mary, at thy window be,
It is the wish'd, the trysted hour!
Those smiles and glances let me see
That make the miser's treasure poor:
How blithely wad I bide the stoure,
A weary slave frae sun to sun;
Could I the rich reward secure,
The lovely Mary Morison.

Yestreen, when to the trembling string,
The dance gaed through the lighted ha',
To thee my fancy took its wing –
I sat, but neither heard nor saw:
Though this was fair, and that was braw,
And yon the toast of a' the town,
I sigh'd, and said, amang them a',
'Ye are na Mary Morison.'

O Mary, canst thou wreck his peace
Wha for thy sake wad gladly die?
Or canst thou break that heart of his
Wha's only faut is loving thee?
If love for love thou wilt na gie,
At least be pity on me shown;
A thought ungentle canna be
The thought o' Mary Morison.

4

COUNTRY GIRL

George Mackay Brown 1921–96

I make seven circles, my love
For your good breaking.
I make the gray circle of bread
And the circle of ale
And I drive the butter round in a golden ring
And I dance when you fiddle
And I turn my face with the turning sun till your
     feet come in from the field.
My lamp throws a circle of light,
Then you lie for an hour in the hot unbroken
     circle of my arms.

5

FALLING IN LOVE

Helena Nelson b. 1953

I didn't believe in falling in love
until I fell in and couldn't get out.
I didn't even have time to shout –
I lost my footing, lost my nerve,
shot head-over-heels down the endless curve
of the helter-skelter some call *lurv.*

You're fifty-four and your hair is thin.
Your polo shirts do not hold mystique
and I am not rich or blonde or chic.
I had no idea it would all begin
with your anxious, apologetic grin
and outstretched hand – but I pulled you in.

It's dark in here, little sense about,
just soupy songs about me and you
and all the revolting words are true.
I'm in lurv with you and in pain without:
They'll write on our headstone, not much doubt,
Fell in, silly sods, and couldn't get out.

6

JOCK O' HAZELDEAN

Sir Walter Scott 1771–1832

'Why weep ye by the tide, ladye?
  Why weep ye by the tide?
I'll wed ye to my youngest son,
  And ye sall be his bride;
And ye sall be his bride, ladye,
  Sae comely to be seen' –
But aye she loot the tears down fa'
  For Jock o' Hazeldean.

'Now let this wilfu' grief be done,
  And dry that cheek sae pale;
Young Frank is chief of Errington,
  And lord of Langley-dale;
His step is first in peacefu' ha',
  His sword in battle keen' –
But aye she loot the tears down fa'
  For Jock o' Hazeldean.

'A chain of gold ye sall not lack,
  Nor braid to bind your hair;
Nor mettled hound nor managed hawk,
  Nor palfrey fresh and fair;
And you, the foremost o' them a',
  Shall ride – our forest queen' –
But aye she loot the tears down fa'
  For Jock o' Hazeldean.

The kirk was deck'd at morning-tide,
    The tapers glimmer'd fair;
The priest and bridegroom wait the bride,
    And dame and knight are there.
They sought her baith by bower and ha';
    The ladye was not seen:
She's o'er the border, and awa'
    Wi' Jock o' Hazeldean.

7

LOVE

Rody Gorman b. 1960

A friend told me
That another friend sends her love

All the way from New Orleans
But that it'll be

Maybe another five weeks
Before it actually arrives.

8

I LO'E NAE A LADDIE BUT ANE

John Clunie 1757–1819

I lo'e nae a laddie but ane,
  He lo'es nae a lassie but me;
He's willing to make me his ain,
  And his ain I am willing to be.
He coft me a rokelay of blue,
  A pair of mittens of green –
The price was a kiss of my mou,
  And I paid him the debt yestreen.

My mither's ay making a phrase,
  That I'm rather young to be wed;
But lang ere she counted my days,
  O' me she was brought to bed.
Sae, mither, just settle your tongue,
  And dinna be flyting sae bauld,
We can weel do the thing when we're young,
  That we canna do weel when we're auld.

coft: bought; *rokelay*: a short cloak

9

THE SHADOWS

Iain Crichton Smith 1928–98

'I think,' she said, 'we shall not see again
each other as we did.' The light is fading
that was once sunny in the April rain.
Across the picture there appears a shading
we didn't notice, but was in the grain.

The picture shows two people happily smiling
with their arms around each other, by the sea.
Whatever they are looking at is beguiling
themselves to themselves. There is a tree
with orange blossoms and an elegant styling

but they are lost quite clearly in each other.
They do not see the landscape, do not hear
the stream that tinkles through the azure weather.
It's as if really the clear atmosphere
were a creation of two souls together.

But at the back there steadily grow two shadows
one for each lover that they can't evade.
They emerge threateningly from the coloured meadows
as if they were a track the two had made
and they were ignorant of, their changeless natures.

And as they move the shades intently follow
growing steadily darker, spreading as they go
as the wings' shades pursue the flying swallow.
My dearest love, if these should make us slow –
remember late the first undying halo.

10

TO HIS MAISTRESS

Alexander Montgomerie c. 1555–98

So swete a kis yistrene fra thee I reft,
In bowing down thy body on the bed,
That evin my lyfe within thy lippis I left;
Sensyne from thee my spirits wald never shed;
To folow thee it from my body fled,
And left my corps als cold as ony ide.
Bot when the danger of my death I dred,
To seik my spreit I sent my harte to thee;
Bot it wes so inamored with thyn ee,
With thee it myndit lykwyse to remane:
So thou hes keepit captive all the thrie,
More glaid to byde then to returne agane.
Except thy breath thare places had suppleit,
Even in thyn armes, thair doutles had I deit.

ide: key

11

THE LAKE AT PREDA

Ron Butlin b. 1949

The stream has ended in a glacier-green transparency of cloud,
blue sky and mountain shadow. We sit down,
we share our wedding-breakfast listening to the water's rush
become accumulated stillness.

When we return next winter the stream will have been silenced
   into ice.
This lake, the scene of our true wedding, will be a sounding-board
set between high mountains
– safe enough to stand on, jump on, dance on.

When we return – what music we will make!

12

BONNY BARBARA ALLAN

Anon

It was in and about the Martinmas time,
  When the green leaves were a falling,
That Sir John Graeme, in the West Country,
  Fell in love with Barbara Allan.

He sent his men down through the town,
  To the place where she was dwelling:
'O haste and come to my master dear,
  Gin ye be Barbara Allan.'

O hooly, hooly rose she up,
  To the place where he was lying,
And when she drew the curtain by.
  'Young man, I think you're dying.'

'O it's I'm sick, and very, very sick,
  And 'tis a' for Barbara Allan:'
'O the better for me ye's never be,
  Tho your heart's blood were a spilling.

'O dinna ye mind, young man,' said she.
  'When ye was in the tavern a drinking.
That ye made the healths gae round and round,
  And slighted Barbara Allan?'

He turnd his face unto the wall.
  And death was with him dealing:
'Adieu, adieu, my dear friends all,
  And be kind to Barbara Allan.'

And slowly, slowly raise she up.
  And slowly, slowly left him,
And sighing said, she could not stay.
  Since death of life had reft him.

She had not gane a mile but twa,
  When she heard the dead-bell ringing.
And every jow that the dead-bell geid,
  It cry'd, Woe to Barbara Allan!

'O mother, mother, make my bed!
  O make it saft and narrow!
Since my love died for me to-day.
  I'll die for him to-morrow.'

13

CHAILL MI MO CHRIDHE RIUT

Ruaridh MacThòmais b. 1921

Chaill mi mo chridhe riut ann an toiseach Màigh,
bha do shliasaid blàth,
teann, mìn, 's ged a b'òigh thu
bha do chìochan làn,
bòidheach fon t-sròl uaine;
agus ann an Òg-mhìos nan uan
laigh mi air t'uachdar,
's cha robh thu air do thruailleadh;
is an uair a thàinig Iuchar
dh'fhaoisgneadh na lusan
is thàinig blàth air a' chanach;
ach thàinig a sin am bruaillean
is fras air na gruaidhean
is mas robh fhios agam dè chanainn
thàinig an lìth donn air a raineach,
's cha robh a chridh agam na chanadh
gun do chaill mi sìoda mìn a' chanaich.

13

I LOST MY HEART TO YOU

Derick Thomson b. 1921

I lost my heart to you at the start of May,
your thighs were warm,
firm and smooth, and though you were a maid
your breasts were full,
beautiful beneath green satin;
and in the lambs' month June
I lay upon you,
and you were not defiled;
and when July came
the buds of the plants burst open
and bloom came on the cotton grass;
but then came anxiety
and tears on cheeks,
and before I knew what to say
a brown tint spread over the bracken,
and I could not say – I had not the heart to do it –
that I had lost the smooth silk of the cotton grass.

14

HEART-FREE

Marion Angus 1854–1944

Sin' noo we twa maun twine
Wi' nae mair troth tae keep
My hert wins oot o' the kist,
Whaur ye lock it it doon sae deep.

My lauch to the laverock gangs,
My grief's fur the hunted hare,
A licht fitstep to the dance,
A kiss at ilka fair.

Here's shoon fur wanton Meg
That ne'er hed hoose nor hame;
A gowden ring fur a nameless lass,
To licht her o' her shame.

The lievin' sall hae my breid,
The corp' my lily-floo'ers,
Some gangrel's bairn the sang o' my lips
I suld hae gi'en to yours.

twine: part; *kist*: box, chest; *lauch*: laugh; *laverock*: lark; *gangrel*: a vagrant, tramp

15

SUITCASES

Kathleen Jamie b. 1962

Piled high in a corner of a second-hand store
in Toronto: of course,
it's an immigrant country. Sometimes

all you can take is what you can carry
when you run: a photo, some clothes,
and the useless dead-weight

of your mother tongue.
One was repaired
with electrician's tape – a trade

was all a man needed. A girl,
well, a girl could get married. Indeed
each case opened like an invitation:

the shell-pink lining, the knicker-
like pockets you hook back
with a finger to look

for the little linked keys.
I remember how each held a wraith
of stale air, and how the assistant seemed

taken aback by my accent;
by then, though, I was headed for home,
bored, and already pregnant.

16

ISLAND LOVE

Tom Pow b. 1950

You walk up from the strand, your creel brimming
with herring; you come down from the hill,
your creel laden with turf, your grey green eyes
cast down on the stony path, your black hair

wet with sweat or a moil of salty mist;
and glad am I there's a bond between us
for it seems to me I'm a poor catch
for this world. My fishing lines tangle and break

in calm waters, lobsters climb from my pots
to go seeking greater challenge elsewhere;
when the sea heaves and gurls black, I'm the first
to lose hope. I set sail with hymns on my lips.

Others there are that would have built for you
a better house; stones that knitted tightly
against the bitter wind, capped with a roof
the hens couldn't lay in. Such men would have turf

stacked for ten winters and then turf to spare;
men to make you proud their knowledge was sought,
their courage praised: for did they not leap
Bull's Cove for you, from black rock to black rock,

as down below fulmars wheeled and the white
water thundered in? They did? God bless them!
But you have a dreamer, a grim fisher
in melancholy; an idler who stares

into the tell-tale smoor of the fire, his tale
often the heaviest creel you carry.
Feckless, your father called me, *indolent*,
your mother: our tongue is rich in name-tags.

Your love is a mystery and a blessing.
No matter where the black dogs take me,
towards overhang or scree, you guide me
back to clear tracks of sunlight; constantly

giving our lives the shape of the journey
they are on. You make plans for the market
and provision for each birth. You let faith
take care of the rest – a deep faith that shines

in those bright grey-green eyes, a faith that sees
the lines of my life when I do not,
that welcomes me dripping from the dark sea
when we give up our tired white bodies with joy.

17

TO MY DAUGHTERS, ASLEEP

Robin Robertson b. 1955

Surrounded by trees I cannot name
that fill with birds I cannot tell apart

I see my children growing away from me;
the hinges of the heart are broken.

Is it too late to start, to late to learn
all the words for love before they wake?

THE SECRET

Elizabeth Burns b. 1957

That the sweet honey of motherlove
is laced with a raw, sour fear
of loss, a fear whose smell
I live with now, knowing that the world
is heavy with it, the air
thick with the stench and ache of it

and I know the other secret,
that underweaving everything
is the web of love that spins between
mothers and their children, this dark and delicate
net that loops us all, encloses us
and holds us fast.

19

LOVE

James Robertson b. 1958

You are there down the flown years,
The dust-blown years, the years
Bundled away like old diaries:
Your name on the pages of diaries
For meetings, movies, meals, arrivals,
Departures; longed for arrivals,
Departures that broke one or other,
Sometimes both of us. Love's like no other
Memory, it cracks anew the heart
When the mind recalls what the heart
Never could forget. You are gone from me,
In touch still but long gone from me
And far from touch. How does time
Flee and yet not move at all? Like the time
I held you in a tiny airless room
Without windows and with room
Just for the mattress we'd made love
On for the last time, the time, my love,
Before you took me for my flight
Away, back home, away, my flight
Away from you and all our grief
And happiness, that room full of grief
And happiness, our hot young tears,
Your face, my face, and our hot young tears.

20

WHEN JOHN AN' ME WAR' MARRIED
Robert Tannahill 1774–1810

When John an' me war' married,
   Our haudin' was but sma',
For my Minnie, canker't carlin,
   Wou'd gie us nocht ava';
I wair't my fee wi' canny care,
   As far as it wou'd gae,
But, weel-I-wat, our bridal bed
   Was clean pea-strae.

Wi' wurkin' late an' early,
   We're come to what ye see,
For fortune thrave aneath our han's,
   Sae eydent ay war' we;
The lowe o' luve made labour light,
   I'm sure ye'll find it sae,
When kind ye cudle down at e'en,
   'Mang clean pea-strae.

The rose blooms gay on cairny brae,
   As weel's in birken shaw,
An' luve will lowe in cottage low,
   As weel's in lofty ha':
Sae lassie tak' the lad ye like,
   Whate'er your Minnie say,
Tho' ye soud mak' your bridal-bed
   O' clean pea-strae.

Minnie: mother; *canker't carlin*: bad-tempered woman; *wair't*: spent; *pea-strae*: pea straw, used as animal bedding; *eydent*: industrious; *lowe:* light, flame; *cairney brae*: stony slope; *birken shaw*: birch forest

21

WALKING GLEN TROOL

Liz Niven b. 1952

There is nothing like
the wind on your face.

You cannot feel it in a prison
or in a hospital.

Neither can you feel it in a cave
looking at spiders.

There is nothing like
the wind in your face.

You cannot feel it when
your mind is locked in sadness

or your heart is broken.
Neither can you feel it when

your senses are dulled by pain
or the corpse lies still in its coffin.

Here, sitting with you,
on the shores of this still loch,

young spring trees greening around us,
and our old love seasoning so well,

we know our good fortune;
feel the wind on our faces.

22

LOVE–MAKING IN ST KILDA

Donald Murray b. 1952

When a man makes love to a St Kildan woman,
her moans and sighs are like the cries of birds –
a cooing and screaming that seems scarcely human
but has been fashioned never to disturb
those who might mistake the sounds their passion makes
for flocks circling Village Bay at night.
Scanning skies for wings when morning breaks,
neighbours wake unaware that soaring flight
had taken place in Main Street's walls
as a man and woman coupled to break free
from an island's bonds and strictures, all
that conspired to tie them down. Gravity
was shed along with trousers, skirt and shawl
as they touched the heights that birds could reach
with their bodies' power and beauty, rise and fall,
arms changed to wings by the tumultuous air they breathed.

23

THE RED GRAVEYARD

Jackie Kay b. 1961

There are some stones that open in the night like flowers
Down in the red graveyard where Bessie haunts her lovers.
There are stones that shake and weep in the heart of night
Down in the red graveyard where Bessie haunts her lovers.

Why do I remember the blues?
I am five or six or seven in the back garden;
the window is wide open;
her voice is slow motion through the heavy summer air.
Jelly roll. Kitchen man. Sausage roll. Frying pan.

Inside the house where I used to be myself,
her voice claims the rooms. In the best room even,
something has changed the shape of my silence.
Why do I remember her voice and not my own mother's?
Why do I remember the blues?

My mother's voice. What was it like?
A flat stone for skitting. An old rock.
Long long grass. Asphalt. Wind. Hail.
Cotton. Linen. Salt. Treacle.
I think it was a peach.
I heard it down to the ribbed stone.

I am coming down the stairs in my father's house.
I am five or six or seven. There is fat thick wallpaper
I always caress, bumping flower into flower.
She is singing. (Did they play anyone else ever?)
My father's feet tap a shiny beat on the floor.

Christ, my father says, that's some voice she's got.
I pick up the record cover. And now. This is slow motion.

My hand swoops, glides, swoops again.
I pick up the cover and my fingers are all over her face.
Her black face. Her magnificent black face.
That's some voice. His shoes dancing on the floor.

There are some stones that open in the night like flowers
Down in the red graveyard where Bessie haunts her lovers.
There are stones that shake and weep in the heart of night
Down in the red graveyard where Bessie haunts her lovers.

24

DUDDINGSTON

Robert Louis Stevenson 1850–94

Now fancy paints that bygone day
    When you were here, my fair –
The whole lake rang with rapid skates
    In the windless, winter air.

You leaned to me, I leaned to you,
    Our course was smooth as flight –
We steered – a heel-touch to the left,
    A heel-touch to the right.

We swung our way through flying men,
    Your hand lay fast in mine,
We saw the shifting crowd dispart,
    The level ice-reach shine.

I swear by yon swan-travelled lake,
    By yon calm hill above,
I swear had we been drowned that day
    We had been drowned in love.

25

LANDSCAPE WITH FLYING MAN

John Glenday b. 1952

I read about him that was given wings.
His father fixed those wings to carry him away.

They carried him half way home, and then he fell.
And he fell not because he flew,

but because he loved it so. You see,
it's neither pride, nor gravity but love

that in the end will pull us back down to the world.
Love furnishes the wings, and that same love

will watch over us as we drown.
The soul makes a thousand crossings; the heart, just one.

A LONG SHOT

Andrew Greig b. 1951

As your lover on waking recounts her dreams,
unruly, striking, unfathomable as herself,
your attention wanders
to her moving lips, throat, those slim shoulders
draped in a shawl of light, and what's being christened here
is not what is said but who is saying it,
the overwhelming fact
she lives and breathes beside you another day.

Other folks' golf shots being even less interesting
than their dreams, I'll be brief:
as she spoke I thought of a putt yesterday at the 4th,
as many feet from the pin as I am years from my birth,
several more than I am from my death –
one stiff clip, it birled across the green,
curved up the rise, swung down the dip
like a miniature planet heading home,

and the strangest thing is not what's going to happen
but your dazed, incredulous knowing it will,
long before the ball reaches the cup then drops,
that it's turned out right after all,
like waking one morning to find yourself
unerringly in love with your wife.

27

ROMANCE

Andrew Lang 1844–1912

My Love dwelt in a Northern land.
A grey tower in a forest green
Was hers, and far on either hand
The long wash of the waves was seen,
And leagues on leagues of yellow sand,
The woven forest boughs between.

And through the silver Northern night
The sunset slowly died away,
And herds of strange deer, lily-white,
Stole forth among the branches grey;
About the coming of the light,
They fled like ghosts before the day.

I know not if the forest green
Still girdles round that castle grey.
I know not if the boughs between
The white deer vanish ere the day.
Above my Love the grass is green.
My heart is colder than the clay.

AMORETTI XIII

John Purser b. 1942

I watched you garden under a dark sky
when cold winter horizontal light
ruffled the crumbled soil and crept round clods
discovering with huge shadows a late fly
or tumbling beetle, busy until night
burying a limp shrew where the brown pods
of broken beans lay flattened in the earth
by piled potato shaws all soft with blight;
and wondered how, in such a sullen time,
you dug tenacious, certain of the worth
of what you did and planting in despite
of all that loss, till the plants climbed
where your love sheltered the young growing part
in the old sheltered garden of the heart.

29

A RONDEL OF LUVE

Alexander Scott c. 1520–c. 1590

Lo! what it is to luve,
Lerne ye, that list to pruve,
Be me, I say, that no wayis may
The grund of greif remuve,
Bot still decay, both nycht and day:
Lo! what it is to luve.

Lufe is ane fervent fyre,
Kendillit without desyre:
Schort plesour, lang displesour;
Repentence is the hyre;
Ane pure tressour without mesour:
Lufe is ane fervent fyre.

To lufe and to be wyiss,
To rege with gud advyiss,
Now thus, now than, so gois the game,
Incertane is the dyiss:
Thair is no man, I say, that can
Both lufe and to be wyiss.

Flee alwayis frome the snair;
Lerne at me to be ware;
It is ane pane and dowbill trane
Of endless wo and cair;
For to refrane that denger plane,
Flee alwayis frome the snair.

Be: by; *pure*: poor; *rege with*: rage at; *dyiss*: dice

30

FHIR LURAICH, 'S FHIR ÀLAINN

Meg Bateman b. 1959

Fhir luraich, 's fhir àlainn,
thug thu dàn dha mo bhilean,

Tobar uisge ghil chraobhaich
a' taomadh thar nan creagan,

Feur caoin agus raithneach
a' glasadh mo shliosan,

Tha do leabaidh sa chanach,
gairm guilbnich air iteig,

Tha ceòban cùbhraidh na Màighe
a' teàrnadh mum thimcheall,

'S e a' toirt suilt agus gutha
dham fhuinn fada dìomhain,

Fhir luraich, 's fhir àlainn,
thug thu dàn dha mo bhilean.

30

BONNIE MAN, LOVELY MAN

Meg Bateman b. 1959

O bonnie man, lovely man,
you've brought a song to my lips,

A spring of clear gushing water
spilling over the rocks,

Soft grasses and bracken
covering my slopes with green,

Your bed is in cotton grass
with curlews calling in flight,

Maytime's sweet drizzle
is settling about me,

Giving mirth and voice
to my uplands long barren,

O bonnie man, lovely man,
you've brought a song to my lips.

31

THE CAUTIOUS LOVER

Sir Alexander Gray 1882–1968

Lassie, lassie, dinna greet!
  Whaur's the sense in bein' wae?
Aye be blithesome when we meet,
  I'll lo'e you yet, but no' the day.
    I like you fine as sure as ocht;
    But mairriagé is a fearsome thocht.

Lassie, lassie, aye believe
  That I'm a douce and honest chiel'.
I'm no' a callant to deceive,
  As a' the clachan kens richt weel.
    There's nane that I can thole but you,
    But mairriage fairly gars me grue.

Lassie, lassie, dinna fear;
  Lippen aye to what I say.
We're only young and losh be here,
  I'll mebbe change my mind some day.
    And though I'm sweir, you needna mind;
    You ken I'm no' the mairryin' kind.

Callant: lad; *lippen*: listen

32

FIRST LOVE

William Neill b. 1922

Well, that was love, and I remember it,
the hope, the hanging round and the heart's pain,
the coolness, coyness and that off-hand bit
that cut my soul and left me scarcely sane.
Now you are fat and forty and quite plain
I can't imagine what it was I saw
that scented night you passed me in the lane
in that lost sunshine springtime long ago.
Time's fairground mirror to a flatter truth
makes nearer passions by comparing pale;
it's just as well first love does not run smooth
but quits the score with a romantic tale.
I loved you dearly, girl who lived next door;
now, cruel heart, I cannot think what for.

33

A RED, RED ROSE

Robert Burns 1759–96

O my luve's like a red, red rose,
That's newly sprung in June:
O my luve's like the melodie
That's sweetly play'd in tune.

As fair art thou, my bonny lass,
So deep in luve am I;
And I will luve thee still, my dear,
Till a' the seas gang dry.

Till a' the seas gang dry, my dear,
And the rocks melt wi' the sun
O I will luve thee still, my dear,
While the sands o' life shall run:

And fare thee weel, my only luve!
And fare thee weel a while!
And I will come again, my luve,
Though it were ten thousand mile.

34

BOUQUET

Angela McSeveney b. 1964

He brought me roses unexpectedly
on our third date
because it was my birthday I thought.

He dropped the knot into my lap casually;
a posy from his garden,
handpicked, the stems bound in tin foil.

There was a full headed red,
three yellows just budding,
one white curled like a soft shell.

Real roses:
thorns, patches of rust,
leathery leaves pocked by insects
and ohh that scent.

I stood them in a glass
at the corner of my bedroom.

In that heavy Summer night
the petals parted without a sound and let go
such a perfume from their discreet pores.

By morning the room
was sweet with it,
the first red petals scattered on the floor.

35

GEORDIE'S MARRIAGE

William Finlayson 1787–1872

O! Ken ye that Geordie and Jean,
  Are cry'd in the Chapel on ither;
And that we are a to convene
  On Friday, to loop them together?
The lassie is handsome an' fair,
  Has plenty o' beauty an' braw-things;
The Villager Gossips declare,
  To plenish a house, she has a' things.

Tho' Geordie has little laid by,
  To serve the important occasion,
Nane need to gang hungry, or dry,
  Gin they hae a stout inclination.
His mither, a pensie auld wife,
  Has vow'd to preside at the table,
And she can plan things to the life,
  When willing, she's hearty, an' able.

Of haggises, lang-kail, an' pies;
  And birsled sheep-heads, there is plenty;
Wi' a patfu' o' guid monie-plies,
  To taste ony mouth that is dainty.
Then, Fiddler, your fiddle-string stent,
  An' play us up *Scamber-come-scratch me;*
This e'enin' on dancing I'm bent,
  Gin the Bridegroom's guid-mother will match me.

pensie: respectable; *lang-kail*: a dish made with Scotch kail

Sae the Fiddler he lilted an' play'd,
  An' the young anes I wat werena idle;
While the Auld Bodies tippled, an' pray'd
  For a blessing to follow this bridal!
But the *Young Folk* deserted the fiel',
  An' skulked unseen frae the Weddin';
Sae some think they'll never do weil,
  As naebody witness'd the Beddin'!

BANNER BRIGHT

Stan Bell b. 1921

Time, love and sharing
have made of us
the warp and weft of
a seamless fabric
made of us the one whole cloth.

Woven tight as any good tweed
stretched between the poles
of a long life
made of us a banner bright.

With memory-symbols
and treasured icons
resplendent as the sun banners
of the Fianna
made of us a woven poem.

Made of us a banner bright.

37

FINDING THE WORDS

Carol Ann Duffy b. 1955

I found the words at the back of a drawer,
wrapped in black cloth, like three rings
slipped from a dead woman's hand, cold,
dull gold. I had held them before,

                    years ago,
then put them away, forgetting whatever it was
I could use them to say. I touched the first to my lips,
the second, the third, like a sacrament,
like a pledge, like a kiss,

               and my breath
warmed them, the words I needed to utter this, small words,
and few. I rubbed at them till they gleamed in my palm –
I love you, I love you, I love you –
as though they were new.

38

CLERK SAUNDERS

Anon

Clerk Saunders and may Margaret
  Walked ower yon garden green;
And sad and heavy was the love
  That fell thir twa between.

'A bed, a bed,' Clerk Saunders said,
  'A bed for you and me!'
'Fye na, fye na,' said may Margaret,
  'Till anes we married be.

'For in may come my seven bauld brothers,
  Wi' torches burning bright;
They'll say, "We hae but ae sister,
  And behold she's wi a knight!"'

'Then take the sword frae my scabbard,
  And slowly lift the pin;
And you may swear, and save your aith.
  Ye never let Clerk Saunders in.

'And take a napkin in your hand,
  And tie up baith your bonny e'en,
And you may swear, and save your aith,
  Ye saw me na since late yestreen.'

---

may: maid; *thir*: these; *anes*: once; *pin*: latch; *een*: eyes

It was about the midnight hour,
  When they asleep were laid,
When in and came her seven brothers,
  Wi' torches burning red.

When in and came her seven brothers,
  Wi' torches burning bright:
They said, 'We hae but ae sister,
  And behold her lying with a knight!'

Then out and spake the first o' them,
  'I bear the sword shall gar him die!'
And out and spake the second o' them,
  'His father has nae mair than he!'

And out and spake the third o' them,
  'I wot that they are lovers dear!'
And out and spake the fourth o' them,
  'They hae been in love this mony a year!'

Then out and spake the fifth o' them,
  'It were great sin true love to twain!'
And out and spake the sixth o' them,
  'It were shame to slay a sleeping man!'

Then up and gat the seventh o' them,
  And never a word spake he;
But he has striped his bright brown brand
  Out through Clerk Saunders' fair bodye.

Clerk Saunders he started, and Margaret she turned
  Into his arms as asleep she lay;
And sad and silent was the night
  That was atween thir twae.

gar: make; *striped*: thrust

And they lay still and sleeped sound
   Until the day began to daw;
And kindly to him she did say,
   'It is time, true love, you were awa'.'

But he lay still, and sleeped sound,
   Albeit the sun began to sheen;
She looked atween her and the wa',
   And dull and drowsie were his e'en.

Then in and came her father dear;
   Said, 'Let a' your mourning be:
I'll carry the dead corpse to the clay,
   And I'll come back and comfort thee.'

'Comfort weel your seven sons;
   For comforted will I never be:
I ween 'twas neither knave nor loon
   Was in the bower last night wi' me.'

The clinking bell gaed through the town,
   To carry the dead corse to the clay;
And Clerk Saunders stood at may Margaret's window,
   I wot, an hour before the day.

'Are ye sleeping, Margaret?' he says,
   'Or are ye waking presentlie?
Give me my faith and troth again,
   I wot, true love, I gied to thee.'

'Your faith and troth ye sall never get,
   Nor our true love sall never twin,
Until ye come within my bower,
   And kiss me cheik and chin.'

---

loon: low-born boy

'My mouth it is full cold, Margaret,
    It has the smell, now, of the ground;
And if I kiss thy comely mouth,
    Thy days of life will not be lang.

'O, cocks are crowing a merry midnight
    I wot the wild fowls are boding day;
Give me my faith and troth again,
    And let me fare me on my way.'

'Thy faith and troth thou sall na get,
    And our true love sall never twin,
Until ye tell what comes of women,
    I wot, who die in strong traivelling?'

'Their beds are made in the heavens high,
    Down at the foot of our good lord's knee,
Weel set about wi' gillyflowers;
    I wot, sweet company for to see.

'O, cocks are crowing a merry midnight,
    I wot the wild fowl are boding day;
The psalms of heaven will soon be sung,
    And I, ere now, will be missed away.'

Then she has ta'en a crystal wand,
    And she has stroken her troth thereon;
She has given it him out at the shot-window,
    Wi' mony a sad sigh, and heavy groan.

'I thank ye, Marg'ret, I thank ye, Marg'ret;
    And aye I thank ye heartilie;
Gin ever the dead come for the quick,
    Be sure, Marg'ret, I'll come for thee.'

traivelling: suffering; *stroken*: struck; *shot-window*: hinged window

It's hosen and shoon, and gown alone,
  She climb'd the wall, and followed him,
Until she came to the green forest,
  And there she lost the sight o' him.

'Is there ony room at your head, Saunders?
  Is there ony room at your feet?
Is there ony room at your side, Saunders,
  Where fain, fain I wad sleep?'

'There's nae room at my head, Marg'ret,
  There's nae room at my feet;
My bed it is full lowly now,
  Amang the hungry worms I sleep.

'Cauld mould is my covering now,
  But and my winding-sheet;
The dew it falls nae sooner down
  Than my resting-place is weet.

'But plait a wand o' bonnie birk,
  And lay it on my breast;
And shed a tear upon my grave,
  And wish my saul gude rest.

'And fair Marg'ret, and rare Marg'ret,
  And Marg'ret, o' veritie,
Gin ere ye love another man,
  Ne'er love him as ye did me.'

Then up and crew the milk-white cock,
  And up and crew the gray;
Her lover vanish'd in the air,
  And she gaed weeping away.

shoon: shoes; *but and*: and also; *birk*: birch

39

YOUR HANDS, THEIR TOUCH
Gael Turnbull 1928–2004

As in a sheltered inlet,
the wind fallen suddenly, all hush,
with pulse of the waves on the naked shingle,
making back and forth, that sound,

so are your hands, their murmuring touch,
in long strokes, wakening tides, no rush,
to surge and carry us, lapped by delight,
in the stillness of one bed.

BITCHEREL

Eleanor Brown b. 1969

You ask what I think of your new acquisition;
and since we are now to be 'friends',
I'll strive to the full to cement my position
with honesty. Dear – it depends.

It depends upon taste, which must not be disputed;
for which of us *does* understand
why some like their furnishings pallid and muted,
their cookery wholesome, but bland?

There isn't a *law* that a face should have features,
it's just that they generally *do*;
God couldn't give colour to *all* of his creatures,
and only gave wit to a few;

I'm sure she has qualities, much underrated,
that compensate amply for this,
along with a charm that is so understated
it's easy for people to miss.

And if there are some who choose clothing to flatter
what beauties they think they possess,
when what's underneath has no shape, does it matter
if there is no shape to the dress?

It's not that I think she is *boring*, precisely,
that isn't the word I would choose;
I know there are men who like girls who talk nicely
and always wear sensible shoes.

It's not that I think she is vapid and silly;
it's not that her voice makes me wince;
but – chilli con carne without any chilli
is only a plateful of mince...

FRACTURE

G. F. Dutton b. 1924

A very small table.
Not even a meal.

Just two glasses on it
both empty and I

am about to explain
there is wine in them still

when you smile and you lean
closer and closer and then

the table is over
and both glasses broken.

No reason for guilt,
nobody's fault,

they are busy with cloths and apologies.
But you have destroyed my metaphor.

And I cannot take my eyes
from your eyes.

42

OF LOVE

Alan Riach b. 1957

If I could bring them all together,
what would I have?

An image of her, smiling in excitement,
approaching in the crowd on London Bridge.

An image of her, thoughtful in her yellow dress,
walking down the grey slope of the street.

And an image of her, at nightfall, hand in hand with me,
crossing the field to a tryst, with kindling fire inside.

And of her, under the tree, laughter light as a bird's wings,
her face, her hands strong as branches.

And of her, standing in the doorway bidding me goodbye.
And of her again, standing in the doorway, returned at last forever.

If I put them all together now, in twenty-seven years,
and called to the ends of the earth, all exultations, fears,

and no predictions count, yet I would say
with certainty: There was love. Now, let it stay.

43

STORM DAMAGE

Tom Leonard b. 1944

There is a stain on the ceiling above the bed.
Rainwater. A relic of last year's storm.
It is roughly circular. Darkest at the centre.
The perimeter is not clearly defined.

Eclipse. Your body moves on mine.
Your face looks down on me.
The lips are smiling. The stain
Becomes a halo round your head.

My mind goes back twelve years.
I am a child again, lying in the grass,
Staring into the sky. Eclipse.

You ask me what I'm thinking.

SAINT VALENTINE'S DAY

William Montgomerie 1904–94

This clear morning let's walk in Rome
together you and I
crossing the *Piazza Flaminia* at the green light
Avanti!
careful of the cars at the *Porta San Valentino*

In the Pincio Gardens
we'll watch *Pulcinella*
and the demon corbies kissing at Nero's tomb

They say the Saint's remains are at *San Prassede's*
here by the Railway Terminal

This afternoon
let's take the *Metropolitana*
past the square Colosseum of the twenty-year empire
to *Ostia Antica*

In the house of Amor and Psyche
I'll share with you
my love
their divine kiss of two millennia
in its box of Roman brick and white marble
set in blue sky

45

THE LOVER

Joe Corrie 1894–1968

Here in the guts of the earth –
    In my father's tomb;
In the forests of aeons past;
    In the gas and the gloom;
Naked, and blind with sweat,
    I strive and I strain;
Helpless, and racked to the heart
    With hate and pain.

But home, I will wash me clean,
    And over the hill,
To the glen of their fair primrose,
    And the daffodil;
And there I will sing of my Love
    So tenderly,
That even the love-lorn gods
    Will envy me.

46

THE RIGS O BARLEY

Robert Burns 1759–96

CHORUS

Corn rigs, an barley rigs,
*   An corn rigs are bonie:*
I'll ne'er forget that happy night,
*   Amang the rigs wi Annie.*

It was upon a Lammas night,
    When corn rigs are bonie,
Beneath the moon's unclouded light,
    I held awa to Annie:
The time flew by, wi tentless heed:
    Till, 'tween the late and early,
Wi sma' persuasion she agreed
    To see me thro the barley.

The sky was blue, the wind was still.
    The moon was shining clearly:
I set her down, wi right good will.
    Amang the rigs o barley:
I ken't her heart was a' my ain;
    I lov'd her most sincerely:
I kiss'd her owre and owre again.
    Amang the rigs o barley.

tentless: careless

I lock'd her in my fond embrace:
    Her heart was beating rarely:
My blessings on that happy place.
    Amang the rigs o barley!
But by the moon and stars so bright.
    That shone that hour so clearly!
She ay shall bless that happy night
    Amang the rigs o barley.

I hae been blythe wi comrades dear:
    I hae been merry drinking:
I hae been joyfu gath'rin gear:
    I hae been happy thinking:
But a' the pleasures e'er I saw,
    Tho three times doubl'd fairly –
That happy night was worth them a'.
    Amang the rigs o barley.

gath'rin gear: making money

47

IN THURSO ONE NIGHT

George Gunn b. 1956

They slip under the eiderdowns of their bodies
the young boys in the bar
resisting their fears & talking about Rangers

when they could be blessed by the soft salt dew
I feel in my hair
this morning as I walked out

to the firth, 'Be strong & then be gentle'
I wanted to cry out to them
'Like those warriors when your country

was young, men who drew their women
to them as lovingly as sheaves of corn
& only put steel through hatred

don't waste your hearts on the tired
organisations of boredom'
That I didn't is part of my general failure

then the night shut like a windblown door
& Thurso seemed
to slide beneath the waves

a Caithness Atlantis
where love comes
from stones

48

OUT WITH MY LOVES ON A WINDY DAY

Pamela Beasant b. 1962

We walked anti-clockwise round the shore path,
defiant, straight through the steel bars of the facing wind;
the hills of Hoy stood near and remote
strips of strong light fanning their dark sides.

My loves and I were walking in the wind
on the very rim of the world.

The rubbled path tickled Alex's feet
and she teetered on sturdy shoes.
She laughed as her hair streamed out,
kicked through her zigzag of interesting wrack;
wondered where the (storm-blown) sand had gone,
felt my coat pocket for polo mints.

Iain, half in and out of his thoughts,
collected firewood, found something for Alex,
ambled bear-like, watchfully, this way and that.
And the *Ola*, wind-caught, shot past Ness Point
in a dogged, lurching mainland dash.

I felt the familiar ferry pang,
Left behind, although I don't really want to go.

We battled through the campsite,
up the South End, past the cannon, red-limbed,
out of breath, till the gale broke
on hard, historical stone.

We had come widdershins to Stromness,
but the town was gracious, it let us pass;
we finished our walk, my loves and I,
came home on a windy day.

THE BLYTHSOME BRIDAL

Sir Frances Sempill c. 1616–82

Fy, let us all to the briddel,
    For there will be lilting there,
For Jockie's to be married to Maggie,
    The lass wi' the gauden hair;
And there will be lang-kail and pottage,
    And bannocks of barley-meal,
And there will be good salt-herring,
    To relish a cog of good ale.
        Fy, let us all to the briddel,
        For there will be lilting there,
            For Jockie's to be married to Maggie,
                The lass wi' the gauden hair. ...

And there will be Sow-libber Peatie,
    And plouckie fac'd Wat in the Mill,
Capper-nos'd Gibbie, and Francie
    That wins in the how of the hill,
And there will be Alaster-Dowgal
    That splee-fitted Bessie did woo,
And sniffling Lillie and Tibbie,
    And Kirstie, that belly-god sow,
        Fy, let us all, &c.

---

lang-kail: unchopped cabbage; *libber*: gelder, castrator

And Crampie, that married Stainie,
    And coft him breeks to his arse,
And afterwards hanged for stealing,
    Great mercy it happened no worse;
And there will be fairntickl'd Hew,
    And Bess wi' the lithe white leg,
That gat to the south for breeding,
    And bang'd up her wame in Mons-Meg.
Fy, let us all, &c. ...

And there will be Girn-again Gibbie,
    And his glaked wife, Jeanie Bell,
And measly chin'd flyting Geordie,
    The lad that was skipper himsell.
There'll be all the lads and the lasses,
    Set down in the midst of the Ha,
With sybows and rifarts and carlings,
    That are both sodden and raw.
Fy, let us all, &c. ...

There will be good lapper'd-milk kebucks,
    And sowens, and farles, and baps,
And swats, and scraped paunches,
    And brandie in stoups and in caps.
And there will be meal-kail and custocks,
    And skink to sup till you rive,
And rosts, to rost on a brander,
    Of flouks that was taken alive.
Fy, let us all, &c.

coft: bought; *fairntickl'd*: freckled; *sybows and rifarts and carlings*: shallots, radishes, brown peas boiled or broiled; *lapper'd-milk kebucks*: cheeses made from curdled milk; *sowens, and farles, and baps*: steeped oats, oatcakes and oven-baked bread; *swats, and scraped paunches*: beer, tripe; *custocks*: cabbage stems; *skink to sup till you rive*: soup made from shin of beef to sup till you burst

Scrap't haddocks, wilks, dulse, and tangle,
    And a mill of good snizing to prie;
When wearie with eating and drinking,
    We'll rise up and dance till we die.
Fy, let us all to the Briddel,
    For there will be lilting there,
For Jockie's to be married to Maggie,
    The lass with the gauden hair.

snizing to prie: snuff to sample

50

THE TIP OF MY TONGUE

Robert Crawford b. 1959

Some days I find, then throw my voice
Deep down the larynx of Glen Esk,

Ears cocked to catch what rumbles back,
English-Scots-Gaelic hailstones.

Other days the tip of my tongue
Is further off than Ayers Rock.

I'm lost for words, or find inside them
A pentecost that isn't tuned in.

I dream I'm a Shetland winterlight
Shining where you drowse in your nightdress,

Dreaming too, your book beside you,
In your hair an aigrette of ferns and beads of rain.

Enough said. Or of waking at a lover's angle
With you on the tip of my tongue.

TRÁIGHEAN

Somhairle MacGill-Eain 1911–96

Nan robh sinn an Talasgar air an tràigh
far a bheil am beul mòr bàn
a' fosgladh eadar dà ghiall chruaidh,
Rubha nan Clach 's am Bioda Ruadh,
sheasainn-sa ri taobh na mara
ag ùrachadh gaoil nam anam
fhad 's a bhiodh an cuan a' lìonadh
camas Thalasgair gu sìorraidh:
sheasainn an siud air lom na tràghad
gu 'n cromadh Preiseal a cheann àigich.

Agus nan robh sinn cuideachd
air tràigh Chalgaraidh am Muile,
eadar Alba is Tiriodh,
eadar an saoghal 's a' bhiothbhuan,
dh'fhuirichinn an siud gu luan
a' tomhas gainmhich bruan air bhruan.
Agus an Uibhist air tràigh Hòmhstaidh
fa chomhair farsaingeachd na h-ònrachd,
dh'fheithinn-sa an siud gu sìorraidh,
braon air bhraon an cuan a' sìoladh.

Agus nan robh mi air tràigh Mhùideart
còmhla riut, a nodhachd ùidhe,
chuirinn suas an co-chur gaoil dhut
an cuan 's a' ghaineamh, bruan air bhraon dhiubh.
'S nan robh sinn air Mol Steinnseil Stamhain
's an fhàirge neo-aoibhneach a' tarraing
nan ulbhag is gan tilgeil tharainn,
thogainn-sa am balla daingeann
ro shìorraidheachd choimhich 's i framhach.

51

SHORES

Sorley MacLean 1911–96
Translated by Iain Crichton Smith

If we were in Talisker on the shore
where the great white foaming mouth of water
opens between two jaws as hard as flint –
the Headland of Stones and the Red Point –
I'd stand forever by the waves
renewing love out of their crumpling graves
as long as the sea would be going over
the Bay of Talisker forever;
I would stand there by the filling tide
till Preshal bowed his stallion head.

And if the two of us were together
on the shores of Calgary in Mull
between Scotland and Tiree,
between this world and eternity,
I'd stand there till time was done
counting the sands grain by grain.
And also on Uist, on Hosta's shore,
in the face of solitude's fierce stare,
I'd remain standing, without sleep,
while sea were ebbing, drop by drop.

And if I were on Moidart's shore
with you, my novelty of desire,
I'd offer this synthesis of love,
grain and water, sand and wave.
And were we by the shelves of Staffin
where the huge joyless sea is coughing
stones and boulders from its throat,
I'd build a fortified wall
against eternity's savage howl.

52

POLYTHERON

Ken Cockburn b. 1960

So hot we sleep with everything open,
doors anchored with stones the beach provided.

A wind that curls behind sends one – slamming
the door to – skittering across the flags.

The white curtain billows into the room
as your breathing lets me know you're asleep;

from the terrace I see a sickle moon
tomorrow's dawn will overtake and wipe

but in today's the animated trees
emerge from night, the morning star lingers

and telephone wires against the pallor
of sky are staves, awaiting notation.

Polytheron: Greek: many-doored, a style of Minoan palace architecture, found at Knossos and elsewhere.

53

MANSIE CONSIDERS PEEDIE MARY
from 'Orkney Lyrics'
Ian Hamilton Finlay 1925–2006

Peedie Alice Mary is
My cousin, so we cannot kiss.
And yet I love my cousin fair:
She wears her seaboots with such an air.

peedie = peerie: little

54

MY LUVE, MY LUVE
from 'Under the Eildon Tree'
Sydney Goodsir Smith 1915–75

My luve, my luve,
Wad ye were here
By me i the touslit bed,
Or wad I had met ye never a day
Or wad ye were aye by me –
Theres nae hauf gaits in love, ye ken.

My luve, my luve.
I wonder wad ye care
To be here by me
I' the Nirvana Oblomovian
Whar is nor nicht nor day
Nor day-o-the-week or year,

Whar nae rain faas,
Sunsheen or sleet or snaw
Nor ocht but an antran tear
In a menner maist Tir-nan-Ogian
Frae the bardic ee
Acause ye arena here.

antran: occasional; *Tir-nan-Ogian*: heavenly

My love, my luve,
Whit havers is this
Gib ye didna ken
And you anerlie
That ahint the bravadie
this hert is near spent.

(The sheer brass neck o the man!)

havers: nonsense; *anerlie*: alone

SEX EDUCATION

Des Dillon b. 1960

Don't wear ski pants nor leggings,
they hug the crotch
and young boys get ideas
from tight crotches.

Isn't that what it's all about?
thought Lynn Marie.

The teacher said:
Don't wear your trousers
too tight around your organ,
young girls won't know
where to put their eyes.

Want a fuckin bet?
thought Lynn Marie.

The teacher said:
Keep to the left in the corridors,
we don't want you all squeezing by.
It's not good for young boys and girls
to be rubbing against each other
in the crush, it makes you aware of things.

You're fuckin right there!
thought Lynn Marie.

56

YEAH YEAH YEAH
Roddy Lumsden b. 1966

No matter what you did to her, she said,
There's times, she said, she misses you, your face
Will pucker in her dream, and times the bed's
Too big. Stray hairs will surface in a place
You used to leave your shoes. A certain phrase,
Some old song on the radio, a joke
You had to be there for, she said, some days
It really gets to her; the way you smoked
Or held a cup, or her, and how you woke
Up crying in the night sometimes, the way
She'd stroke and hush you back, and how you broke
Her still. All this she told me yesterday,
Then she rolled over, laughed, began to do
To me what she so rarely did with you.

57

THE PROPOSAL

John C. Milne 1897–1962

Ye'll get hens that'll keckle a' winter,
Birns o' reid-kamed cocks,
Hame-ower turkeys that gobble,
And reid-luggit bubbly-jocks;

Rich ream-bannocks and butter,
Sweet-milk kebbucks o' cheese,
And honey as clear as yer een, lass,
Fae three muckle skeps o' bees;

The best biggit hoosie in Buchan
That sits on the tap o' the brae,
And sheets o' my mither's great-granny's –
Od, lassie, fut mair wad ye hae!

---

birns: loads; *hame-ower*: homely; *reid-luggit*: red-eared; *bubbly-jocks*: turkey-cocks; *ream-bannocks*: oatmeal-cakes made with cream; *kebbucks o' cheese*: home-made cheeses; *skeps o' bees*: the contents of a bee-hive

58

HOT CHICK

Sheila Templeton b. 1941

Ma man sez
'Yer... HOT'
Ah sez 'Mmm'
in his ear.
He sez 'Naw
yer HOT, ah mean
sizzlin', hen, ah
could fry an egg
oan yer back.
Whit's wrang,
ur ye no weel?
It's no verra comfy
fur me.
Yerr like a toasty
hot water bottle
a' the time.
Iz this whit thon
Germaine Greer
cries the Change?
Ur you huvven
a hot flush?'

'Naw,' ah sez,
'Ah'm huvven
a Power Surge.
An' you kin sleep
on the flerr.'

59

BALLAD

William Soutar 1898–1943

O! shairly ye hae seen my love
Doun whaur the waters wind:
He walks like ane wha fears nae man
And yet his e'en are kind.

O! shairly ye hae seen my love
At the turnin o' the tide;
for then he gethers in the nets
Doun be the waterside.

O! lassie I hae seen your love
At the turnin o' the tide;
And he was wi' the fisher-folk
Doun be the waterside.

The fisher-folk were at their trade
No far frae Walnut Grove;
They gether'd in their dreepin nets
And fund your ain true love.

60

THE LOWLANDS OF HOLLAND

Anon

My love has built a bonny ship, and set her on the sea,
With seven score good mariners to bear her company;
There's three score is sunk, and threescore dead at sea,
And the lowlands of Holland has twin'd my love and me.

My love he built another ship, and set her on the main,
And nane but twenty mariners for to bring her hame,
But the weary wind began to rise, and the sea began to rout,
My love then and his bonny ship turn'd withershins about.

There shall neither coif come on my head, nor comb come in my hair;
There shall neither coal nor candle light shine in my bower mair,
Nor will I love another one, until the day I die,
For I never lov'd a love but one, and he's drown'd in the sea.

O haud your tongue my daughter dear, be still and be content,
There are mair lads in Galloway, ye need nae sair lament;
O! there is nane in Galloway, there's nane at a' for me,
For I never lov'd a love but ane, and he's drown'd in the sea.

61

SANG

Robert McLellan 1907–85

There's a reid lowe in yer cheek,
Mither, and a licht in yer ee,
And ye sing like the shuilfie in the slae,
But no for me.

The man that cam the day,
Mither, that ye ran to meet,
He drapt his gun and fondlet ye
And I was left to greit.

Ye served him kail frae the pat,
Mither, and meat frae the bane.
Ye brocht him cherries frae the gean,
And I gat haurdly ane.

And nou he lies in yer bed,
Mither, and the licht growes dim,
And the sang ye sing as ye hap me ower
Is meant for him.

lowe: flame; *shuilfie*: chaffinch; *slae*: sloe; *gean:* wild cherry tree; *hap*: cover

62

SO, WE'LL GO NO MORE A ROVING

George Gordon, Lord Byron 1788–1824

So, we'll go no more a roving
    So late into the night,
Though the heart be still as loving,
    And the moon be still as bright.

For the sword outwears its sheath,
    And the soul wears out the breast,
And the heart must pause to breathe,
    And love itself have rest.

Though the night was made for loving.
    And the day returns too soon,
Yet we'll go no more a roving
    By the light of the moon.

63

CUPID AND VENUS

Mark Alexander Boyd 1563–1601

Fra banc to banc, fra wod to wod I rin,
Ourhailit with my feble fantasie,
Like til a leif that fallis from a trie
Or til a reid ourblawin with the win'.
Twa gods gydes me; the ane of them is blin –
Yea, and a bairn brocht up in vanitie –
The nixt a wyf ingenrit of the sea,
And lichter nor a dauphin with hir fin.

Unhappie is the man for evirmaire
That teils the sand and sawis in the aire;
Bot twyse unhappier is he, I lairn,
That feidis in his hairt a mad desyre,
And follows on a woman throw the fyre,
Led be a blind and teichit be a bairn.

ourhailit: oppressed; *ourblawin*: blown over; *ingenrit*: born, engendered;
dauphin: dolphin; *teils*: tills

64

OTHER LIFE
Brian McCabe b. 1951

I lie in the darkness and listen
to some threadbare life in our room,

some fretful other life in our room
– it isn't me it isn't you –

at times like a breathless trust
or the spatter of a hesitant rain;

caresses of feverish shadows;
asthma of a dying candle

– it isn't you it isn't me –
can't you hear it there it is again:

a sparse stirring of the wind
in the branches of a leafless tree.

You say: It's just
the jenny-long-legs, that's all.

I know. Though even that
sounds more description than name.

In my cupped hand it is
some scarce yearning grown restless:

a desire searching for a gesture;
a love looking for its word.

65

O, WERT THOU IN THE CAULD BLAST

Robert Burns 1759–96

O, wert thou in the cauld blast
    On yonder lea, on yonder lea,
My plaidie to the angry airt,
    I'd shelter thee, I'd shelter thee.
Or did Misfortune's bitter storms
    Around thee blaw, around thee blaw,
Thy bield should be my bosom,
    To share it a', to share it a'.

Or were I in the wildest waste,
    Sae black and bare, sae black and bare,
The desert were a Paradise,
    If thou wert there, if thou wert there.
Or were I monarch o the globe,
    Wi thee to reign, wi thee to reign,
The brightest jewel in my crown
    Wad be my queen, wad be my queen.

airt: direction of the wind; *bield*: shelter

66

THE THREAD

Don Paterson b. 1963

Jamie made his landing in the world
so hard he ploughed straight back into the earth.
They caught him by the thread of his one breath
and pulled him up. They don't know how it held.
And so today I thank what higher will
brought us to here, to you and me and Russ,
the great twin-engined swaying wingspan of us
roaring down the back of Kirrie Hill

and your two-year-old lungs somehow out-revving
every engine in the universe.
All that trouble just to turn up dead
was all I thought that long week. Now the thread
is holding all of us: look at our tiny house,
son, the white dot of your mother waving.

67

DÒMHNALL NAN DÒMHNALL
Gun urra

Thug mi sùil thar a' bhealaich, thug mi 'n sealladh ud bhuam,
dh'fheuch am faicinn mo leannan tighinn dhan bhaile san uair,
fhir a dh'òladh an togsaid 's a chostadh a luach –
's math thig bonaid ghorm dhathte air cùl bachlach nan dual.

B' fheàrr gu faicinn a-nuas thu 's do ghruaidh mar an ròs
agus d' anail mar ùbhlan 's do chùl mar an t-òr;
do bheul tha dearg tana, 's blas na meal' air do phòig –
gura gìomanach eal' thu agus lach air an lòn.

O,'s èibhinn gach àite am biodh pàirt de Chlann Nìll,
gura h-uasal gach òigear leis an òlte am fìon,
air chairtean ag iomairt gun mhionnan gun strì –
gur ann làmh riutha shuidhinn is gu leiginn mo sgìths.

Gura bòidheach, gura bòidheach, gura bòidheach na lòin,
gura bòidheach an t-aonach air an sgaoileadh an ceò;
gura bòidheach an Losaid 's Baile Ghrobain na còir,
gura bòidheach Ceann Loch far 'm bi mo sheachd rùn ag òl.

Dè! Nam biodh tu mar shionnach air an tulaich ud thall
agus mise mar eala air bharraibh nan tonn,
Nàile, rachainn ad choinneamh agus mheallainn thu leam,
lùb ùr a' chùil chlannaich, ort tha m' anam an geall.

A Dhòmhnaill nan Dòmhnall, sùil mhòdhar ad cheann –
Rìgh, gur math thig dhut triubhas dhol a shiubhal nan gleann,
's cha mhios' thig dhut stocaidh, bròg shocair 's i teann;
's tric a laigh mi ri d' thaobh, 's ann leam a b' aobhach bhith ann.

DONALD OF THE DONALDS

Anon

Translated by Meg Bateman

I looked beyond the pass, I looked all about,
to see if my sweetheart was yet coming home.
You could drink a barrel and pay for its cost;
well does a blue bonnet suit your ringleted curls.

I hoped to see you descending, your cheek like the rose,
your breath apple-scented and your hair like gold,
your lips, red and slender, your honey-tasting kiss,
of swans you are a hunter and of duck on the flood.

Delightful every place that belonged to Clan Neil,
noble every youth who would drink the wine
while gaming at cards without swearing or strife,
I'd go over to sit with them to recover my cheer.

Lovely, lovely, lovely the fields,
lovely the peaks where mist would disperse,
lovely is Losaid and Baile Ghroban close by,
lovely is Kinloch where my sevenfold love drinks.

If you on yonder hillock were like a fox,
and I like a swan on the crests of the waves,
I'd set out to meet you and you I'd entice;
fresh locks of curling hair, you have captured my soul.

Oh, Donald of the Donalds, gentle the eye in your head,
you look good in trews going to travel the hills,
no less good in a stocking, and a soft neat shoe,
often I lay down beside you, and that was my joy.

68

LUVE

Douglas Young 1913–73

Gie aa, and aa comes back
 wi mair nor aa.
Hain ocht, and ye'll hae nocht,
 aa flees awa.

Hain ocht: keep anything; *hae nocht*: have nothing

69

HUSBANDRY

John Burnside b. 1955

Why children make pulp of slugs
with a sprinkling of salt

or hang a nest of fledglings on a gate
with stolen pins

is why I sometimes turn towards the dark
and leave you guessing,

only to know the butter and nickel taste
of cruelty;
          to watch, and show no sign

of having seen.
          Not
wickedness, that sometimes celebrates

a tightness in the mind;
but what I comprehend

of fear and love:
cradled remoteness, nurtured by stalled desire;

willed deprivation;
the silence I'm learning by heart.

70

WHEESHT, WHEESHT
Hugh MacDiarmid 1892–1978

Wheesht, wheesht, my foolish hert,
For weel ye ken
I widna ha'e ye stert
Auld ploys again.

It's guid to see her lie
Sae snod an' cool,
A' lust o' lovin' by –
Wheesht, wheesht, ye fule!

snod: neatly laid out

71

BETWEEN

Hamish Whyte b. 1947

I lie awake
listening to the wind.
There are metaphors
and metaphors but none
to give a roof to this longing
for my new love.
The house creaks slightly.
There is no ghost here
only the absence
of my old love.

72

THE COMING OF LOVE
from The Kingis Quair
King James I of Scotland 1394–1437

Bewailing in my chamber thus allone,
  Despeired of all joye and remedye,
Fortirit of my thoght, and woebegone,
  Unto the window gan I walk in hye
  To se the warld and the folk that went forby.
As, for the tyme, though I of mirthis fude
Myght have no more, to luke it did me gude.

Now was there maid fast by the touris wall
  A gardyn faire, and in the corneris set
Ane herbere grene with wandis long and small
  Railit about; and so with treis set
  Was all the place, and hawthorn hegis knet,
That lyf was none walking there forby
That myght within scarse ony wight aspye:

So thik the bewis and the leves grene
  Beschadit all the aleyes that there were.
And myddis every herber myght be sene
  The scharp, grene, swete jenepere,
  Growing so faire with branchis here and there,
That, as it semyt to a lyf without,
The bewis spred the herbere all about. ...

quair: book; *fortirit*: tired; *gan*: began; *herbere*: arbour; *wight*: man; *bewis*:
boughs; *aleyes*: alleys; *myddis*: amidst; *jenepere*: juniper

And therewith kest I doune myn eye ageyne,
  Quhare as I sawe walking under the tour,
Full secretly new cummyn hir to pleyne,
  The fairest or the freschest yong floure
  That ever I sawe, me thoght, before that houre;
For quhich sodayn abate anone astert
The blude of all my body to my herte.

And though I stude abaisit tho a lyte,
  No wonder was – for quhy, my wittis all
Were so ouercom with plesance and delyte
  – Onely throu latting of myn eyen fall –
  That sudaynly my hert became hir thrall
For ever, of free wyll, for of manace
There was no takyn in hir swete face.

And in my hede I drew ryght hastily,
  And eftsones I lent it forth ageyne
And saw hir walk, that verray womanly,
  With no wight mo bot onely wommen tweyne.
  Than gan I studye in myself and seyne:
'A, swete, ar ye a warldly creature,
Or hevinly thing in liknesse of nature?

'Or ar ye god Cupidis owin princesse
  And cummyn ar to louse me out of band?
Or ar ye verray Nature the goddesse
  That have depaynted with your hevinly hand
  This gardyn full of flouris, as they stand?
Quhat sall I think? Allace, quhat reverence
Sall I minister to your excellence?

pleyne: play, be amused; *sodayn abate anone astert*: suddenly with-drew, then
returned; *abaisit*: abashed; *lyte*: little; *manace*: menace; *takyn*: token; *eftsones*:
soon after; *tweyne*: two; *band*: bondage

'Gif ye a goddesse be, and that ye like
    To do me payne, I may it noght astert.
Gif ye be warldly wight that dooth me sike,
    Quhy lest God mak you so, my derrest hert,
    To do a sely prisoner thus smert,
That lufis yow all, and wote of noght bot wo?
And therefor, merci, swete, sen it is so!'

astert: escape; *dooth me sike*: makes me sigh; *sely*: feeble; *wote*: knows

73

FOR HER SAKE

Alastair Reid b. 1926

Her world is all aware. She reads
omens in small happenings, the fall of a teaspoon,
flurries of birds, a cat's back arching,
words unspoken, wine spilt.
She will notice moods in handwriting,
be tuned to feelings in a room,
sense ill luck in a house, take heed of ghosts,
hear children cry before the sound has reached her,
stay unperturbed in storms, keep silence
where speech would spoil. Days are her changes,
weather her time.

Whether it be becalmed in cool mornings
of air and water, or thunderstruck through nights
where flesh craves and is answered, in her, love
knows no division, is an incarnation
of all her wonder, as she makes
madness subside, and all thought-splintered things
grow whole again.

Look below. She walks in the garden,
preoccupied with paths, head bent,
beautiful, not at rest, as objects are,
but moving, in the fleck of light and shade.
Her ways are hers, not mine. Pointless to make
my sense of her, or claim her faithfulness.

She is as women are, aware
of her own mystery, in her way faithful
to flowers and days; and from the window's distance,
I watch her, haunted by her otherness.

Well to love true women, whose whims are wise,
whose world is warm, whose home is time,
and well to pleasure them, since, last of all,
they are the truth which men must tell,
and in their pleasure, houses lighten,
gardens grow fruitful, and true tales are told.
Well to move from mind's distance
into their aura, where the air
is shifting, intimate, particular.

And of true women, she, whose eyes illumine
this day I wake in – well to mark
her weather, how her look is candid,
her voice clear-toned, her heart private,
her love both wild and reticent.
Well to praise and please her, well to make
this for her sake.

SCOPS OWL

Anna Crowe b. 1945

Tonight I lie without you
under a pelt of darkness
heavy with cypress
ragged with goat-cries.

Under the white moon's Roman coin
dogs are barking from distant farms
with little rips of sound
that stone walls catch, throw back.

All this he draws like silk
through a gold ring
into a single woodwind note,
tongued and sweet –

a true and level fluting
I picture travelling
through night's horizons
north, to where you sleep.

75

THE BAFFLED KNIGHT

Anon

There was a knight, and he was young,
  A riding along the way, sir,
And there he met a lady fair,
  Among the cocks of hay, sir.

Quoth he, 'Shall you and I, lady,
  Among the grass lye down a?
And I will have a special care
  Of rumpling of your gown a.'

'If you will go along with me
  Unto my father's hall, sir,
You shall enjoy my maidenhead,
  And my estate and all, sir.'

So he mounted her on a milk-white steed,
  Himself upon another,
And then they rid upon the road,
  Like sister and like brother.

And when she came to her father's house,
  Which was moated round about, sir,
She stepped straight within the gate,
  And shut this young knight out, sir.

'Here is a purse of gold,' she said,
  'Take it for your pains, sir;
And I will send my father's man
  To go home with you again, sir.

'And if you meet a lady fair,
  As you go thro the next town, sir,
You must not fear the dew of the grass,
  Nor the rumpling of her gown, sir.

'And if you meet a lady gay,
  As you go by the hill, sir,
If you will not when you may,
  You shall not when you will, sir.'

WHY IT TOOK SO LONG

Diana Hendry b. 1941

You were otherwise occupied
and so, in a thistledown way, was I.
Also, living in the wrong town
and not done with the lunacies of youth
or the worse ones of middle age.
There were children, of course,
taking priority in energy, money, love,
and tenderising of the heart to be done
and all the impedimenta of history,
fantasy, expectation to ditch,
and the barbed-wire brambles to snip,
and the breast plate to strip,
and the look-out to drug,
and one's mother to silence,
and one's cover to blow,
and one's heart to risk.

Even so, when my waist was slim
and my hair still brown,
where were you?

77

O TELL ME HOW TO WOO THEE

Robert Graham c. 1750–97

If doughty deeds my ladye please,
  Right soon I'll mount my steed;
And strong his arm, and fast his seat,
  That bears frae me the meed.
I'll wear thy colours in my cap,
  Thy picture in my heart;
And he that bends not to thine eye,
  Shall rue it to his smart.

    Then tell me how to woo thee, love;
      O tell me how to woo thee!
    For thy dear sake, nae care I'll take,
      Tho' ne'er another trow me.

If gay attire delight thine eye,
  I'll dight me in array;
I'll tend thy chamber door all night,
  And squire thee all the day.
If sweetest sounds can win thy ear,
  These sounds I'll strive to catch;
Thy voice I'll steal to woo thysel',
  That voice that nane can match.

---

meed: prize; *trow*: trust; *dight me in array*: dress and adorn myself

Then tell me how to woo thee, love;
  O tell me how to woo thee!
For thy dear sake, nae care I'll take,
  Tho' ne'er another trow me.

But if fond love thy heart can gain,
  I never broke a vow;
Nae maiden lays her skaith to me,
  I never loved but you.
For you alone I ride the ring,
  For you I wear the blue;
For you alone I strive to sing,
  O tell me how to woo!

skaith: harm

78

SHY GEORDIE

Helen Cruickshank 1886–1975

Up the Noran Water
In by Inglismaddy,
Annie's got a bairnie
That hasna got a daddy.
Some say it's Tammas's,
An' some say it's Chay's;
An' naebody expec'it it,
Wi' Annie's quiet ways.

Up the Noran Water
The bonnie little mannie
Is dandled an' cuddled close
By Inglismaddy's Annie.
Wha the bairnie's daddy is
The lassie never says;
But some think it's Tammas's,
An' some think it's Chay's.

Up the Noran Water
The country folk are kind;
An' wha the bairnie's daddy is
They dinna muckle mind.
But oh! the bairn at Annie's breist,
The love in Annie's e'e –
They mak' me wish wi' a' my micht
The lucky lad was me!

79

A NIGHT IN

Liz Lochhead b. 1947

Darling, tonight I want to celebrate
not your birthday, no, nor mine.
It's not the anniversary of when we met,
first went to bed or got married, and the wine
is supermarket plonk. I'm just about to grate
rat-trap cheddar on the veggie bake that'll do us fine.

But it's far from the feast that – knowing you'll be soon,
and suddenly so glad to just be me and here,
now, in our bright kitchen – I wish I'd stopped and gone
and shopped for, planned and savoured earlier.
Come home! It's been a long day. Now the perfect moon
through our high windows rises round and clear.

JUST LIKE EVE

Magi Gibson b. 1947

I could have brought you
whisky to warm you on winter nights,
poems full of words to fill your silences

I could have brought you
armfuls of flowers
to fill your rooms with summer,
scented petals to scatter where you dream

I could have brought
olives, shiny, black and green,
anchovies and Parmesan,
Chianti, deep blood-red

I could have brought
figs, dates, kumquats, lychees
tastes to make your senses sing
to set your soul adrift

Instead I brought
forbidden fruit
the one and only gift
you would not accept

81

AA MY THOCHTS

(*All mein Gedanken*. Bavarian folksong, c. 1460)

J. K. Annand 1908–93

Aa the thochts that eir I hae, are thochts o ye.
My ane and only solace, be ye aye true to me!
Ye, ay, ye, soud hain me in your hert.
Gif I had my dearest wish
We twa wad never ever pairt.

My ane and only solace, think ye on this, my ain,
My life and gear will aye be yours alane to hain.
Yours, ay, yours, sall I forever be,
Ye are my smeddum and my joy,
Frae sorrow ye can make me free.

thochts: thoughts; *soud hain*: should hold; *gif*: if; *gear*: posessions; *smeddum*:
energy, spirit

82

VIVAMUS MEA LESBIA ATQUE AMEMUS

*(after Catullus, Gaius Valerius, 84–c. 54*BC*)*
Hamish Henderson 1919–2002

for Gayle, on her birthday

Noo Gayle, my dear, ye maunna fear
The snash o' dour auld bodies O.
It's daft to miss a single kiss
Tae please sic muckle cuddies O.

Live while ye may, and lo'e the day –
In life there's naething certain O.
Oor peerie licht sune ends in nicht,
When Fate rings doon the curtain O.

Sae kiss me mair – and mair – and mair:
A thoosan kisses gie me O.
– But dinna count the haill amount
Lest a' my senses lea me O.

---

snash: sneers, gibes; *muckle cuddies*: great idiots; *peerie*: small; *lea*: leave

83

THE LOCH NESS MONSTER

Tom Buchan 1931–95

Sometimes at night when the wind blows hard
the Loch Ness monster is lonely
for his extinct contemporaries
the warm flying fox and the luscious algae

so too in the long silent hours when the wind blows
(the black water closing over my head)
I am lonely for you my extinct love
pinioned down there in the strata

'I love you' I cry –
but you cannot weep or move your head

and I am terrified I shall not be near you again
until the rocks are broken
and our dead dust is blown out into space.

84

LAMENT OF THE BORDER WIDOW

Anon

My love he built me a bonny bower,
And clad it a' wi' lilye flour;
A brawer bower ye ne'er did see,
Than my true love he built for me.

There came a man, by middle day,
He spied his sport, and went away;
And brought the King that very night,
Who brake my bower, and slew my knight.

He slew my knight, to me sae dear;
He slew my knight, and poin'd his gear;
My servants all for life did flee,
And left me in extremitie.

I sew'd his sheet, making my mane;
I watch'd the corpse, myself alane;
I watch'd his body, night and day;
No living creature came that way.

I took his body on my back,
And whiles I gaed, and whiles I sat;
I digg'd a grave, and laid him in,
And happ'd him with the sod sae green.

lilye: pale yellow; *making my mane*: lamenting

But think na ye my heart was sair,
When I laid the moul' on his yellow hair?
O think na ye my heart was wae,
When I turn'd about, away to gae?

Nae living man I'll love again,
Since that my lovely knight is slain;
Wi' ae lock of his yellow hair
I'll chain my heart for evermair.

85

IN THE LANE

Isobel Wylie Hutchison 1889–1982

I met two lovers in the lane
    Sheepish and shy,
I met two lovers in the lane
    And passed them by.

Oh! It's a lovely thing to be
    A lover or his lass,
And it is lovely to be free
    And look and pass.

CREATURES

Douglas Dunn b. 1942

A lime tree buzzed with its remembered bees.
We stood on the terrace. Fanatic prayers
Rattled with resigned displeasure. Martyrs!
'Ave!' Grasshoppers. Insect rosaries.

Nervously proud, itself, and secular,
A fox patrolled on its instinctive route
Past us and nut trees to the absolute
Wild pathless woods, a French fox, pure *renard*.

Hérisson and the encyclopaedic owl
Plotted the earth and sky of dusk. Oldest
Inhabited valley – we felt it blessed
By creatures and impacted human soul.

She said, 'The world is coming out tonight.'
Vézère's *falaises* moved grey; an ivied mist
Disguised the distance and we stood, our trust
In lizards, settling birds, the impolite

Belettes, the heavy hornets and the truths
Compiling in our senses, plain, of this life,
If inarticulate. I loved my wife.
Our two lives fluttered like two windowed moths.

She was the gentlest creature of them all.
She scattered milk-dipped bread for the lazy snakes
Asleep in the Mouliniers' bramble-brakes.
I asked her, 'Why?' 'It's only natural.'

A paradisal stasis filled the dark.
She scattered bread. 'A snake's a shy creature.'
I dip my bread in milk, and I think of her,
The châtelaine of her reasonable ark.

87

ORAN LUAIDH

Aonghas MacNeacail b. 1942

bha gealach a-nochd ann
cobhar geal air an tràigh

b'àill leam thu
bhith còmhla rium

clach-mheallain a-nise
sgleogadh air m'uinneig

b'àill leam thu
bhith còmhla rium

sgal-osag mun cuairt
mo bhothan air chrith

b'àill leam thu
bhith còmhla rium

m'amharc an dràst'
air fàire do-fhaicsinn

b'àill leam thu
bhith còmhla rium

sàl is talamh
crìon is sìorraidh

b'àill leam thu
bhith còmhla rium

fàd air teine
thu 'nam chridhe

b'àill leam thu
bhith còmhla rium

a' chruinne bhith
fo ghul is cràdh

b'àill leam thu
bhith còmhla rium

ùir is salann
corp is anam

b'àill leam thu
bhith còmhla rium

'na mo dhùsgadh
'na mo bhruadar

b'àill leam thu
bhith còmhla rium

LOVESONG/WAULKING SONG

Aonghas MacNeacail b. 1942

a bright moon tonight shone
white foam on the shore

love that you
were here with me

a flurry of hail now
slaps at my window

love that you
were here with me

shrill gust around
my trembling hut

love that you
were here with me

now i search
obscured horizons

love that you
were here with me

brine and soil
short-lived, eternal

love that you
were here with me

burning peat is
you my heart's fire

love that you
were here with me

the world may all be
steeped in anguish

love that you
were here with me

earth and salt
body, spirit

love that you
were here with me

in my waking
in my sleeping

love that you
were here with me

88

CONTINENT O VENUS

Alexander Scott 1920–89

She liggs ablow my body's lust and luve,
A country dearlie-kent, and yet sae fremd
That she's at aince thon Tir-nan-Og I've dreamed,
The airt I've lived in, whar I mean tae live,
And mair much mair, a mixter-maxter wand
Whar fact and dream are taigled up and snorled.

I ken ilk bay o aa her body's strand,
Yet ken them new ilk time I come tae shore,
For she's the unchartit sea whar I maun fare
Tae find anither undiscovered land,
Tae find it fremd, and yet tae find it dear,
Tae seek for't aye, and aye be bydan there.

liggs: lies; *fremd*: foreign; *Tir-nan-Og*: Gaelic Paradise; *airt*: quarter

89

Gerry Cambridge b. 1959

O, Miss Aphrodite Saltcoats
Is the girl for me,
She makes most men get out their boats
And sail upon the sea.

She paints her nails, shapely, long,
In delicatest shade of pink,
And laughs, and sings a little song
Of men who cannot think:

O Aphrodite, I am done
With thought, the finest say;
Let us retire to eat the sun,
And fold away the day;

Many a room, through you, is bare,
And many a tear is shed,
Started by that flesh you wear,
And many a heart in dread.

O Aphrodite, Aphrodite,
Take your silk blouse off for me:
I'll stop being high and mighty,
Nor venture on the sea.

90

TAM I' THE KIRK

Violet Jacob 1864–1946

O Jean, my Jean, when the bell ca's the congregation
O'er valley and hill wi' the ding frae its iron mou',
When a'body's thochts is set on their ain salvation,
    Mine's set on you.

There's a reid rose lies on the Buik o' the Word afore ye
That was growin' braw on its bush at the keek o' day,
But the lad that pu'd yon flower i' the mornin's glory
    He canna pray.

He canna pray, but there's nane i' the kirk will heed him
Whaur he sits sae still his lane at the side o' the wa',
For nane but the reid rose kens what my lassie gied him –
    It and us twa.

He canna sing for the sang that his ain he'rt raises,
He canna see for the mist that's afore his een,
And a voice droons the hale o' the psalms and the paraphrases
    Crying 'Jean! Jean! Jean!'

91

LOVE'S REMORSE

Edwin Muir 1887–1959

I feel remorse for all that time has done
To you, my love, as if myself, not time,
Had set on you the never-resting sun
And the little deadly days, to work this crime.

For not to guard what by such grace was given,
But leave it for the idle hours to take,
Let autumn bury away our summer heaven:
To such a charge what answer can I make

But the old saw still by the heart retold,
'Love is exempt from time.' And that is true.
But we, the loved and the lover, we grow old;
Only the truth, the truth is always new:

'Eternity alone our wrong can right,
That makes all young again in time's despite.'

92

SONNET

Mary, Queen of Scots 1542–87 (attrib.)
From *'Mon amour croist, et plus en plus croistra'*,
translated by James Robertson

My love grows, and yet mair on mair shall grow
As lang as I hae life: O happy pairt,
Alane tae haud a place in that dear hairt
Tae which in time my love itsel shall show
Sae clear that he can nane misdoot me then!
For him I will staun stieve agin sair fate,
For him I will strive for the heichest state,
And dae sae muckle for him he shall ken
I naething hae – nae gowd, nae gear, nae pleisure –
But tae obey and serve him in haill meisure.
For him I hope for aw guid chance and graith;
For him I will me keep baith quick and weel;
True smeddum I desire for him and feel,
And niver will I change while I hae braith.

nane misdoot me: doubt me not at all; *stieve*: strong, sturdy; *heichest*: highest;
gowd: gold; *graith*: wealth, possessions; *smeddum*: spirit, courage

93

QUEEN MARY, QUEEN MARY

Anon (Singing game)

Queen Mary, Queen Mary, my age is sixteen,
My father's a farmer on yonder green:
He's plenty of money to dress me sae braw –
But nae bonnie laddie will tak' me awa'.

I rose in the morning, I looked in the glass,
I said to myself 'What a handsome young lass!'
My hands by my side, and I gave a 'Ha-ha!' –
Come awa', bonnie laddie, and tak' me awa'.

94

INCIDENT

Norman MacCaig 1910–96

I look across the table and think
(fiery with love)
Ask me, go on, ask me
to do something impossible,
something freakishly useless,
something unimaginable and inimitable

like making a finger break into blossom
or walking for half an hour in twenty minutes
or remembering tomorrow.

I will you to ask it.
But all you say is
Will you give me a cigarette, please?
And I smile and,

returning to the marvellous world
of possibility,
I give you one
with a hand that trembles
with a human trembling.

GLEN ISLA LOVE SONG
Valerie Gillies b. 1948

from Òran le Fear Chrannard an Gleann Ìle
by The guidman of Crandart

'S mòr mo mhulad 's cha lugh' m' èislein,
ge b' e dh'èisteadh rium;

's tric mi 'g amharc thar a' bhealaich,
's m' air' air dol a-nunn.

(*Verses 1 and 2*)

My longing wastes me with its yearning,
Whoever will listen to me, hear

How often I'm looking up at the high pass
With my mind on travelling over Monega!

Late at night I'm longing to go
To that glen on the far side

Where the blue-eyed girl will be,
The shapely one with the long blonde hair.

Through the great pineforest on a pitchblack night
I'd go, under a downpour of heavy rain.

I'd swim across without oar, without oak,
If my love were on the other shore.

The river headlong in spate cannot hold me back
    Even if my stepping-stone goes under the wave.

I'll give that girl there a lovely shirt
    With silk at the cuffs of the sleeves,

And she'll give me a patterned crossbelt
    Richly diced and studded with silver.

Love overwhelms me for the girl by the Mar fir,
    The girl with the level gaze.

                    * * *

I'll be in misery if you're going to marry another
    While I'm kept up country among the bens.

No gap in my teeth, not a wrinkle on my face,
    There's never a wheeze in my chest;

You won't give me up for any weakness
    But for the sharp company of the lowlanders.

I don't know much about sowing barley
    Yet I'll provide young goats for you,

You'll get a stag from the high slope, a trout from the pool,
    And the antlered roebuck of the cairns,

The brindled mallard, the greylag of the western isles,
    And the swan of most elegant swimming,

A red bird of the dark moors, the grey hen's whitebelt son,
    And the handsome steed of the wood, the capercaillie.

If I owned everything as far as Lochaber
And even further beyond, with maybe

Elgin o' Moray and Edinburgh along with it
And all the lands in between,

They'd count for nothing, I'd reject them all
Before I would give up our pledge.

96

LASSIE LIE NEAR ME

Anon

Lang hae we parted been
Lassie, my dearie;
Now we are met again,
Lassie, lie near me.

Near me, near me,
Lassie, lie near me,
Lang hast thou lein thy lain,
Lassie, lie near me.

I LEAVE THIS AT YOUR EAR

W. S. Graham 1918–86

For Nessie Dunsmuir

I leave this at your ear for when you wake,
A creature in its abstract cage asleep.
Your dreams blindfold you by the light they make.

The owl called from the naked-woman tree
As I came down by the Kyle farm to hear
Your house silent by the speaking sea.

I have come late but I have come before
Later with slaked steps from stone to stone
To hope to find you listening for the door.

I stand in the ticking room. My dear, I take
A moth kiss from your breath. The shore gulls cry.
I leave this at your ear for when you wake.

98

JOHN ANDERSON MY JO, JOHN
Robert Burns 1759–96

John Anderson my jo, John,
When we were first acquent;
Your locks were like the raven,
Your bonny brow was brent;
But now your brow is beld, John,
Your locks are like the snow;
But blessings on your frosty pow,
John Anderson my jo.

John Anderson my jo, John,
We clamb the hill thegither;
And mony a canty day, John,
We've had wi' ane anither:
Now we maun totter doun, John,
And hand in hand we'll go,
And sleep thegither at the foot,
John Anderson my jo.

jo: darling; *brent*: high and straight; *beld*: bald; *pow*: head; *canty*: merry

99

SONNET ON MY WIFE'S BIRTHDAY

George Bruce 1909–2002

All the love I have will not take her years away:
All the knowledge given not grant her time release,
Yet one day less impoverishes this great feast
That grew when we together went our way,
Hurrying to meet our newly planted day,
That barely showed above the stony ground
Of our North-East, whose grudging air beat down
The rare freedom that becomes when two are one.
So, when every loss is gain, as every colour, brown
Or red or tarnished yellow in our life's spectrum,
Shows itself, why should we protest too much
Against the silent pace that makes in us such
Speed, for we have learned to plant our love so strong
Our children's children now take up the song.

100

THERE WILL BE NO END

Anne MacLeod b. 1951

There will be no end to the joy, my love.
We will stand together as the stars
sweep the Cuillin, rounding into morning
the bright new morning of the tender heart.
And where we sing, the song will be a fine one
and where we dance, our steps will never fail
to tap the spring of life, of love and laughter
timeless as stars, the wheeling, circling stars
that dance and sing, and sing and dance again:
and there will be no end
to the joy

NOTES

1   **JAMES HOGG** was the son of a shepherd in Ettrick, in the Borders. At 15 he bought a fiddle to play at weddings and fairs, and shortly after began writing poetry. In 1810 he came to Edinburgh, where as one of Scott's circle he gained recognition for his poetry and stories. *The Private Memoirs and Confessions of a Justified Sinner* is his masterpiece. This quatrain is from a poem written to the tune 'Paddy's Wedding'.

2   **EDWIN MORGAN** was born in Glasgow and educated at the University of Glasgow where he became a lecturer in English, retiring as Professor in 1980. Appointed Glasgow's Poet Laureate in 1999 and Scotland's National Poet in 2004, his eclectic output spans *Collected Translations*, Scots versions of *Cyrano de Bergerac* and *Phèdre*, *New Selected Poems* (2000), and *A Book of Lives* and *Beyond the Sun, (*2007).

3   **ROBERT BURNS** was born in Alloway, Ayrshire. The Kilmarnock edition of 1786, with its comic and satiric poems, saw the first flowering of his genius. In 1788 he married Jean Armour. Attempts at farming failing he joined the Excise in Dumfries where, plagued by money troubles and ill-health, he died aged 37. He dismissed this early piece as 'not very remarkable either for its merits or its demerits'. The title was probably chosen for euphony. (See also numbers 33, 46, 65 and 98.)

4   **GEORGE MACKAY BROWN** was born in Stromness, Orkney and studied at Newbattle College and Edinburgh University. His distinctive output includes 'A Calendar of Love' and 'A Time to Keep' (stories), *Magnus* and *Greenvoe* (novels), an autobiography, many volumes of poems and posthumously, *Orkney Pictures and Poems* (with Gunnie Moberg, 1996) and *Collected Poems* (2005).

5   **HELENA NELSON** is a poet, critic and editor. She runs Happen-
       Stance Press and edits *Sphinx,* dedicated to chapbook poetry.
       Her collections include *Mr and Mrs Philpott on Holiday in
       Auchterawe & Other Poems* (2002), *Starlight on Water* (2003)
       and *Unsuitable Poems* (2005).

6   **SIR WALTER SCOTT** was born in Edinburgh. Frail as a child, he
       was looked after by grandparents near Kelso. These early years
       and the lore and history of the Borders deeply influenced his
       writing, including his long narrative poems 'The Lay of the
       Last Minstrel' and 'Marmion', and gave rise to his *Minstrelsy of
       the Scottish Border*. Turning to prose fiction, he effectively
       invented the historical novel. The start of this poem is from
       the ballad of John of Hazelgreen.

7   **RODY GORMAN** was born in Dublin and lives on the Isle of
       Skye. He writes in Scottish and Irish Gaelic and in English,
       and teaches at Sabhal Mòr Ostaig. His most recent collections
       include *On the Underground/Air a' Charbad fo Thalamh* (2000),
       Naomhóga na Laoi (2003) and *An Guth 3* (editor, 2005).

8   **JOHN CLUNIE** was the minister of Ewes. He provided Burns
       (who saw him as 'a worthy little fellow of a clergyman') with
       the words of 'Ca' the yowes to the knowes'. The opening of
       this poem was purloined by Hector Macneill, who added four
       indifferent stanzas of his own.

9   **IAIN CRICHTON SMITH** was born in Glasgow and grew up on
       Lewis. After studying at Aberdeen University he taught in
       Clydebank and Oban. His prolific output spanned poetry, nov-
       els, stories, and plays, in English and Gaelic. After his *Collected
       Poems* of 1992 came *The Leaf and the Marble* (1998) and *A
       Country for Old Men* (2000). His complete stories and 'Murdo'
       works came out in 2001.

10 **ALEXANDER MONTGOMERIE** was born at Hessilhead Castle near Beith, Ayrshire, and was reputed to have resided for a time in Galloway. The foremost member of the 'Castalian Band' of poets at the court of James VI, and last of the grand generation of makars, he is best known for 'The Cherry and the Slae'. His Catholicism, first employed by James in secret dealings with Philip of Spain, led finally to exile and outlawry.

11 **RON BUTLIN** lives in Edinburgh, and in 2008 was appointed the city's Makar. His prose publications include the novels *The Sound of my Voice* and *Belonging*, and *No More Angels* (short stories). Among his poetry collections are *Ragtime in Unfamiliar Bars* (1985), *Histories of Desire* (1995) and *Without a Backward Glance: New and Selected Poems* (2005). He is also an opera librettist.

12 **ANON**, 'Bonny Barbara Allan'. No. 84 in Child's collection, and prior to that from *The Tea-Table Miscellany* (1763), edited by Allan Ramsey. Attitudes towards it seem ambivalent, and it has been drily noted that the ballad has shown more staying power than its 'spineless lover'.

13 **RUARAIDH MACTHÒMAIS / DERICK THOMSON** was born on Lewis and attended the Universities of Aberdeen and Cambridge. From 1963 to 1991 he held the chair of Celtic Studies at Glasgow. Scholar and critic, and founder-editor of the Gaelic literary journal *Gairm,* his published poetry includes a collected volume *Creachadh na Clàrsaich/Plundering the Harp* (1982), *Sùil air Fàire/Surveying the Horizon* (2007) and *Meall Garbh/The Rugged Mountain* (1995).

14 **MARION ANGUS** grew up in Arbroath and lived most of her life in Aberdeen. Becoming a poet after the First World War when she was 50, she claimed she 'would rather have a humble place among the poets of the Nor' East than a seat with the Mighty'. Her *Selected Poems* appeared in 1950; while she and Violet Jacob share *Voices From Their Ain Countrie* (2006).

15   **KATHLEEN JAMIE** was born in the west of Scotland, and lives in Fife. Her poetry includes *The Queen of Sheba* (1994), *Jizzen* (1999), *Mr and Mrs Scotland are Dead: Selected Poems* (2002) and *The Tree House* (2004). *Among Muslims* (2002) recounts travels in Northern Pakistan, and *Findings* (2005) her journeys in Scotland and discoveries in the natural world. She teaches Creative Writing at the University of St Andrews.

16   **TOM POW** is from Edinburgh and lives in Dumfries. He is Head of Creative and Cultural Studies at Glasgow University's Crichton Campus. Poetry collections include *The Moth Trap* (1990), *Red Letter Day* (1996), *Landscapes and Elegies* (2004), *Sparks!* (with Diana Hendry, 2005) and *Dear Alice: Narratives of Madness* (2008). He has written radio plays, a travel work about Peru, and novels for children.

17   **ROBIN ROBERTSON** is from Scone, Perthshire. His poetry collections include *A Painted Field* (1997), *Slow Air* (2002) and *Swithering* (2006). He edited *Mortification: Writers' Stories of Their Public Shame*. He lives in London. Having done editorial work at Penguin, and developed a poetry list for Secker and Warburg, he is currently a literary editor at Jonathan Cape.

18   **ELIZABETH BURNS** grew up in Edinburgh and having spent much of her life in Scotland, now lives in Lancaster where she teaches creative writing. Her poetry collections include *Ophelia and other poems* (1991), *The Gift of Light* (1999) and *The Lantern Bearers* (2007).

19   **JAMES ROBERTSON** lives in Newtyle, Angus where he runs the pamphlet imprint Kettillonia and is general editor of Itchy Coo, the Scots language publisher for schools and young people. His novels are *The Fanatic*, *Joseph Knight* and *The Testament of Gideon Mack*. His poetry includes *Sound-Shadow* (1995), *Stirling Sonnets* (2001) and *Voyage of Intent* (2005, after a residency at the Scottish Parliament).

20 **ROBERT TANNAHILL** was born in Paisley and apprenticed to his father, a weaver. Latterly he lived with his mother. In 1807 his only book, a verse drama with 33 'other poems and songs, chiefly in the Scottish dialect', appeared by subscription. In 1810 a new ms was rejected; and on 17 May he committed suicide in the Candren Burn, his coat and silver watch being found on the bank nearby.

21 **LIZ NIVEN** grew up in Glasgow and studied at Glasgow University and Jordanhill Training College. Now in Dumfries, she is a consultant on the use of the Scots language in Education. TV programmes on her work include 'Haud Yer Tongue' and 'Poet on a Plane'. Among her poetry collections are *Stravaigin* (2001) and *Burning Whins and other poems* (2004).

22 **DONALD MURRAY** is from Ness, on the Isle of Lewis. After a spell in Benbecula he now lives in Shetland and teaches English. Besides his poetry, he has published a short story collection, *Special Deliverance*.

23 **JACKIE KAY** grew up in Glasgow and lives in Manchester. Among her collections of poems are *The Adoption Papers* (1991), *Other Lovers* (1993), *Life Mask* (2005) and *Darling: New and Selected Poems* (2007). She publishes prose, and poetry for children; and writes regularly for stage, television and radio. In 1992 Sphinx Theatre produced her play about Bessie Smith, *Every Bit of It*.

24 **ROBERT LOUIS STEVENSON** was born in Edinburgh. Rather than follow his father into engineering he took up law, becoming an advocate in 1875. On holiday in France he met Fanny Osbourne, his future wife. After South Seas trips for his health, they settled in Samoa. He is famed for his tales of travel and adventure, *Kidnapped* and *Treasure Island*, and *Dr Jekyll and Mr Hyde*. He wrote poems for adults (*Underwoods*) and children (*A Child's Garden of Verses*).

25   **JOHN GLENDAY** was born in Monifieth, Angus. Educated at the University of Edinburgh he was for 12 years a psychiatric nurse in Dundee. He now lives in Carnoustie and works as a drugs counseller. His poetry publications include *The Apple Ghost* (1989) and *Undark* (1995).

26   **ANDREW GREIG** was born in Bannockburn, Stirling. He lives in Orkney and Peebles. His most recent poetry collections are *Into You* (2001) and *This Life, This Life: New & Selected Poems 1970–2006* (2007). Other publications include his novels *In Another Light* and *Romanno Bridge*, two chronicles of his Himalyan expeditions, and *Preferred Lies*, about life, mortality, golf and Scotland.

27   **ANDREW LANG** was born in Selkirk and educated at St Andrews. Most of his working life was spent in London as a journalist and essayist. Like Stevenson (whom he met there) he went as an invalid to the Riviera, his first book of poems containing ballads and lyrics of Old France. He also wrote versions of fairy stories for children.

28   **JOHN PURSER** was born in Glasgow. His poetry collections are *The Counting Stick* (1976), *A Share of the Wind* (1980) and *Amoretti* (1985). He has published a study of Jack B. Yeats, and is known as a composer and author of radio plays, including *Carver*. His book and radio series *Scotland's Music* had a dual impact, an enlarged edition of the former coming out in 2007. He lives and crofts on the Isle of Skye.

29   **ALEXANDER SCOTT** is said to have been from Dalkeith, his association with the Erskine family taking him to France and the court of the young Queen Mary. The musicality of many of his poems in the Bannatyne Ms would complement claims that he was the organist at the Augustinian priory of Inchmahome, in the Firth of Forth. Much of his later work displays a gloomy hue, in the wake of his wife leaving him.

30 **MEG BATEMAN** was born in Edinburgh and educated at Aberdeen University where she also taught. She now lives on Skye, teaching at Sabhal Mòr Ostaig and working as a reviewer and translator in both Gaelic and English. Her poetry publications are *Orain Ghaoil* (1991), *Aotromachd agus Dàin Eile/Lightness and Other Poems* (1997), and *Soirbheas/Fair Wind* (2007).

31 **SIR ALEXANDER GRAY** was born in Dundee and studied at the Universities of Edinburgh, Göttingen and Paris. After a spell in the Civil Service he became Professor of Political Economy in Aberdeen and Edinburgh. He drew on North-East Scots in his own poems and his translations of ballads and folksongs, mainly from Danish and German.

32 **WILLIAM NEILL** is an Ayrshireman born and bred. Having studied Celtic Studies and English at the University of Edinburgh, he writes in all three Scottish languages, Scots, English and Gaelic. His *Selected Poems 1969–1992* appeared in 1994, and *Caledonian Cramboclink* in 2001. He lives in Galloway.

33 **ROBERT BURNS** (ii) 'A Red, Red Rose' is a perfect illustration of Burns's genius for reworking folk material (almost every line here was taken from a patchwork of black-letter ballads and popular broadsheets) to produce one of the great love songs of our literature.

34 **ANGELA MCSEVENEY** grew up in Ross-shire, Livingstone and the Borders. In 1982 she moved to study in Edinburgh, where she still lives and works as a care assistant. Her collections of poetry are *Coming Out With It* (1992), *Imprint* (2002) and *Slaughtering Rhubarb* (2008).

35 **WILLIAM FINLAYSON** was born in Pollokshaws, Glasgow and became secretary to the weavers' union some time after 1810. For fifty years from 1822 he worked (as Burns did, latterly) as an exciseman. He died in Leith in 1872. 'Geordie's Marriage'

appeared in his *Simple Scottish Rhymes,* published in Paisley in 1815.

36   **STAN BELL** was born and lives in Glasgow. He studied at The Glasgow School of Art where he subsequently taught. His publications include *The First President*, a monograph on the political significance of R. B. Cunninghame Graham and most recently *In Search of Stansylvania: forty-two poems* (2006).

37   **CAROL ANN DUFFY** was born in Glasgow and studied philosophy at Liverpool University. A poet, dramatist and anthologist, she lives in Manchester and is Creative Director of the Writing School at Manchester Metropolitan University. Among her poetry collections are *The Other Country* (1990), *The World's Wife* (1999), *Feminine Gospels* (2002) and *Rapture* (2005), and for children, *The Hat* (2007).

38   **ANON**, 'Clerk Saunders'. Combining Child 69A and 77B ('Sweet William's Ghost') this tale of doomed love was first published in 1802 by Scott who took it from Herd's Ms but making emendations. The last three stanzas, not always included, vividly round off the tragic story.

39   **GAEL TURNBULL** was born in Edinburgh, where he returned after spending most of his working life as a doctor in England, Canada and the States. His individualistic, often experimental poetry publications include *From the Language of the Heart* (1985), *Transmutations* (1997), *A Rattle of Scree* (1997), *Might a shape of words* (2000) and *There are Words: collected poems* (2006).

40   **ELEANOR BROWN** grew up in Scotland. She has subsequently lived in France, and is now in Hertfordshire. Her appropriately titled debut collection *Maiden Speech* was published in 1996. Her version of Sophocles' *Philoctetes* was staged at the Cockpit Theatre in London.

41   **G. F. DUTTON** is of Scottish ancestry, and lives in Perthshire. His activities as a research scientist, mountaineer, swimmer and 'marginal' gardener are documented in numerous publications. His poetry collections include *Squaring the Waves* (1986), *The Concrete Garden* (1991) and *The Bare Abundance: Selected Poems 1975–2001* (2002).

42   **ALAN RIACH** was born in Airdrie, and educated at Cambridge and Glasgow. After holding a professorship at Waikato University, New Zealand he returned to Glasgow University and is currently Professor of Scottish Literature. He edited Hugh MacDiarmid's collected works. His poetry includes *An Open Return* (1991), *First & Last Songs* (1995), *Clearances* (2001) and *Scotlands: Poets and the Nation* (ed).

43   **TOM LEONARD** was born in Glasgow. *Intimate Voices* and *access to the silence* constitute his *Collected Poems 1965–2004*. Author of critical essays and plays, and of the biographical study *Places of the Mind: The Life and Work of James Thomson (B. V.)*, he also compiled the anthology *Radical Renfrew: Poetry from the French Revolution to the First World War*. He teaches Creative Writing at Glasgow University.

44   **WILLIAM MONTGOMERIE** was born in Glasgow, the son of a Plymouth Brethren evangelist. His poetry includes *Via* (1933), *Squared Circle* (1934) and *From Time to Time: Selected Poems* (1985). He and his wife Norah collected a unique library of books and recordings of traditional Scottish rhymes, tales and games. *The Folk Tales of Scotland* was reissued in 2008.

45   **JOE CORRIE** grew up in the mining community of Bowhill, in Fife. His dramatic output was prolific, his most highly regarded full-length play *In Time of Strife* depicting the effect of the 1926 General Strike on miners and their families. *Joe Corrie: Plays, Poems and Theatre Writings* was published in 1985.

46   **ROBERT BURNS** (iii) 'The Rigs o Barley', composed around 1742 from an old song, joyously captures the moment of surrender to passion. Anne Rankine, daughter of a farming neighbour near Lochlie, claimed in later life to have been the girl. But this is apparently very dubious.

47   **GEORGE GUNN** was born in Thurso where he still lives. He has been a deep-sea fisherman, a driller for oil and a journalist. He is also a playwright and Artistic Director of Grey Coast Theatre Company, which he co-founded in 1992. His poetry publications include *Black Fish* (2004) and *Winter Barley* (2005).

48   **PAMELA BEASANT** is from Glasgow and lives in Stromness. She has written for children, and a biography of Stanley Cursitor. Her poetry collection *Running with a Snow Leopard* appeared in 2008, as did *A New Orkney Anthology*, edited by her as George Mackay Brown Writing Fellow.

49   **SIR FRANCIS SEMPILL** was born in Beltrees, Renfrewshire, studied law and became Sheriff-Depute of Renfrewshire. This rumbustious piece, with its graphic depiction of the wedding-guests and the dishes they so grossly tucked into, has been aptly compared to one of Breughel's peasant feasts.

50   **ROBERT CRAWFORD** was born in Lanarkshire. His poetry collections include *A Scottish Assembly* (1990), *The Tip of My Tongue* (2003), *Selected Poems* (2005) and *Full Volume* (2008). He co-edited *The Penguin Book of Scottish Verse.* His critical studies include *Scotland's Books: The Penguin History of Scottish Literature.* He is professor of Modern Scottish Literature at the University of St Andrews.

51   **SOMHAIRLE MACGILL-EAIN/SORLEY MACLEAN** was born on Raasay. After studying at Edinburgh University and fighting in North Africa during World War II, he was for many years head teacher at Plockton High School. His first book was *Dàin do*

Eimhir agus Dàin Eile/Poems to Eimhir and Other Poems (1943). A collected volume *O Choille gu Bearradh/From Wood to Ridge* was published in 1999. Translation by Iain Crichton Smith (see 9)

52   **KEN COCKBURN** was born in Kirkcaldy, and studied in Aberdeen and Cardiff. From 1996 to 2004 he worked at the Scottish Poetry Library in Edinburgh, one of his projects being the CD *Jewel Box*. He jointly established and ran pocketbooks; and is an editor and translator. His collections include *Souvenirs and Homelands* (1998), *Feathers and Lime* (translations) (2007) and *On the flyleaf* (2007).

53   **IAN HAMILTON FINLAY** was born in the Bahamas, and grew up in Glasgow and Orkney. He founded the Wild Hawthorn Press and edited *Poor.Old.Tired.Horse*. At Stonypath in Lanarkshire he created Little Sparta, a classical garden in the 18th century tradition, as a critique of contemporary culture. *The Dancers Inherit the Party and Glasgow Beasts an a Burd* (2004) contains a selection of his stories and poetry.

54   **SYDNEY GOODSIR SMITH** was born in New Zealand. He studied medicine, briefly, at Edinburgh University, and history at Oriel College, Oxford. He adopted mediaeval Scots, and its archaisms, in his own work. His volumes from *Skaill Wind* (1941) to *Gowdspink in Reekie* (1975) are represented in *Collected Poems* (1975). He also published a verse play, *The Wallace* and a novel, *Carotid Cornucopius*.

55   **DES DILLON** was born in Coatbridge. He studied at Strathclyde University and with Open University. He has taught, been Castlemilk's Writer in Residence, and now lives in Galloway. Best known as a prose writer and dramatist his first book, *Sniz* (1994), was a collection of poetry; and *Picking Brambles and Other Poems* came out in 2003.

56 **RODDY LUMSDEN** was born in St Andrews. After a spell in Edinburgh he moved to London, and is currently a tutor at City University and Morley College. His poetry collections include *Yeah Yeah Yeah* (1997), *The Book of Love* (2000) and *Mischief Night: New & Selected Poems* (2004). Besides being a poetry critic and website commentator, he is a puzzle and popular reference writer.

57 **JOHN C. MILNE** grew up on an Aberdeenshire farm. He took three first-class honours degrees at Aberdeen University. Much of *The Orra Loon* (1946), the one book published in his lifetime, depicts farm folk and customs. Further work which he hoped to publish on his retirement appeared posthumously in *Poems* (1963, reissued 1976).

58 **SHEILA TEMPLETON** was born in Aberdeen, prior to a childhood ranging from Rannoch Moor to Dar-es-Salaam. She lives in Troon. Her first collection is *Slow Road Home* (2004), and she is one of the Makar Poets, a live performance collective who share the anthology *Running Threads* (2006). She also writes fiction for adults and children.

59 **WILLIAM SOUTAR** was born in Perth. He wrote in Scots both for adults and for children. While in the Navy during World War I he contracted spondylitis. He graduated from Edinburgh University but, his health worsening, his last thirteen years were bedridden. *Diaries of a Dying Man* came out in 1954 and *Into a Room: selected poems* in 2000.

60 **ANON**, 'The Lowlands of Holland'. The text of this broadside ballad is taken from Volume II of David Herd's 1769 collection of *Scottish Songs, Heroic Ballads &c.*

61 **ROBERT MCLELLAN** grew up on his grandparents' Lanarkshire farm. From 1938 he lived on Arran, the setting for *Sweet Largie Bay* (1956) and *Arran Burn* (1965), written for television.

The best-known of his plays in Scots are *Jamie the Saxt* and *The Flouers o' Edinburgh*; and he enjoyed popular success with his *Linmill Stories* and radio work.

62 **GEORGE GORDON, LORD BYRON** was born in London but schooled in Aberdeen. On inheriting his title he went to Harrow and Cambridge. As a member of the Romantic movement he gained celebrity with his narrative poems 'Childe Harold's Pilgrimage', 'Don Juan' and 'A Vision of Judgement'. In 1823 he joined the Greek insurgents who had risen against the Turks, but died of marsh fever before seeing military action.

63 **MARK ALEXANDER BOYD** was born in Penkill, Ayrshire, studied law in Paris, Orleans and Bourges before plague drove him to Italy, and fought for Henry III in the French civil war. His wanderings are described in his letters. This Italianate sonnet, his sole surviving poem not written in Latin, is considered one of the finest love-poems in Scottish literature.

64 **BRIAN MCCABE** was born near Edinburgh and studied at Edinburgh University where he was appointed Writer in Residence in 2005. His poetry collections are *Spring's Witch* (1984), *One Atom to Another* (1987) and *Body Parts* (1999), and his prose works include a novel, *The Other McCoy*, and *Selected Stories*. He currently edits *The Edinburgh Review*.

65 **ROBERT BURNS** (iv) 'O Wert Thou in the Cauld Blast' was addressed to Jessie Lewars, who helped nurse him in his last illness. A few weeks before his death she played her favourite tune 'Lenox Love to Blantyre' on the piano for him: he wrote these poignant words for the melody.

66 **DON PATERSON** moved from Dundee to London to pursue a musical career, returning in 1993 as Writer in Residence to Dundee University. He later worked in London as a composer, guitarist, editor and writer until becoming a lecturer in Creative

Writing at the University of St Andrews. Poetry includes *Nil Nil* (1993), *God's Gift to Women* (1997), *The Eyes* (1999), *Landing Light* (2003) and *Orpheus* (2006). Among his other publications are two books of aphorisms.

67   **ANON**, 'Dòmhnall nan Dòmhnall/Donald of the Donalds'. This traditional piece follows bardic custom in its robust praise of the beloved. The original was made by a woman from Kintyre, the source of its place-names. It appears in the 1848 collection of Dòmhnall Rothach (Donald Munro). Translation by Meg Bateman (see 30).

68   **DOUGLAS YOUNG** was born in Fife and spent his early childhood in India. Schooled in Edinburgh he studied at St Andrews and Oxford. After lecturing here he held chairs in Classics and Greek in Canada and North Carolina. He published three collections of poems, with a selected volume in 1950. He translated from Gaelic, and transmogrified Aristophanes into Scots ('The Burdies', 'The Puddocks').

69   **JOHN BURNSIDE** was born in Dunfermline and lives in Fife. He is Reader in Creative Writing at the University of St Andrews. His poetry collections include *The Myth of the Twin* (1994), *The Asylum Dance* (2000), *The Light Trap* (2002) and *Good Neighbour* (2005), with his *Selected Poems* appearing in 2006. Among prose works are *Burning Elvis* (short stories), a memoir, *A Lie About My Father*, and novels.

70   '**HUGH MACDIARMID**' (**C. M. GRIEVE**) was born in Langholm and after war service settled in Montrose as a journalist. Scotland's most influential writer of the 20th century, he urged the regeneration of all aspects of Scottish life and culture. *A Drunk Man Looks at the Thistle* is cited as the masterwork of modern Scottish poetry. Since his *Complete Poems Vol. 1* (1993) further volumes of poetry and prose have appeared.

71 **HAMISH WHYTE** was born near Glasgow and was for many years a librarian. He now lives in Edinburgh. Poetry collections include *Christmasses* (1998), *A Bird in the Hand* (2008) and *Mungo's Tongues* (editor). He runs Mariscat Press, has co-edited *New Writing Scotland*, and is an Honorary Research Fellow in the Scottish Literature Department, Glasgow University.

72 **KING JAMES I OF SCOTLAND** was captured by the English in 1406, while sailing to France, and held captive until 1424. It is claimed he wrote 'The Kingis Quair' (197 stanzas of rhyme-royal in Scots, but influenced by Chaucer) near the end of this period, in Windsor Castle, to celebrate his falling in love with Lady Jane Beaufort, who became his queen. The earliest ms dates from 1475, 38 years after James's brutal murder at Perth.

73 **ALASTAIR REID** was born in Whithorn and graduated from the University of St Andrews after war service in the navy. He has lived in Europe, the USA, and Central and South America. For many years a staff writer for *The New Yorker,* he is an essayist, chronicler and translator – especially of Neruda and Borges. *Weathering* appeared in 1978, *Oases* in 1999, and *Inside Out and Outside In* (his selected prose, poetry and translations) in 2008.

74 **ANNA CROWE** was born in Devonport and since 1986 has lived in St Andrews. She co-founded and was director of the StAnza poetry festival. Her publications include *Skating out of the House* (1997), *A Secret History of Rhubarb* (2004), *Punk with Dulcimer* (2006), *Joan Margarit: Tugs in the Fog* (translator) and *Lights Off Water* (editor).

75 **ANON,** 'The Baffled Knight'. Identified also as 'The Shy Shepherd' and 'Blow away the morning dew...', this cheerily admonitory piece appears in this form as No. 112B in Child's collection.

76   **DIANA HENDRY** lives in Edinburgh. Her poetry collections are *Making Blue* (1995), *Borderers* (2001), *Twelve Lilts: Psalms & Responses* (2003) and *Sparks!* (with Tom Pow, 2005). Her books for children include *Harvey Angell* and *You Can't Kiss it Better*. She has been a journalist, creative writing tutor and Writer in Residence at Dumfries and Galloway Royal Infirmary.

77   **ROBERT GRAHAM** was from Gartmore. After spending the bulk of his life in Jamaica as Receiver-General he became Lord Rector of Glasgow University (1785) and MP for Stirlingshire. A memoir of him (*Doughty Deeds*) was written by his grandson, the writer and adventurer R. B. Cunninghame Graham.

78   **HELEN CRUICKSHANK** left school in Angus at 15, for economic reasons. She was a civil servant, for ten years in London, then in Edinburgh. Her poetry collections were *Up the Noran Water* (1934), *Sea Buckthorn* (1954), *The Ponnage Pool* (1968) and *Collected Poems* (1970). Her posthumous *Octobiography* appeared in 1976.

79   **LIZ LOCHHEAD** is from Lanarkshire, and was educated at Glasgow School of Art. Poetry includes *Dreaming Frankenstein* (1983) and *The Colour of Black & White* (2003). Her stage plays range from *Blood and Ice*, *Mary Queen of Scots Got Her Head Chopped Off* and *Perfect Days* to *Miseryguts* (from *Le Misanthrope*) and *Educating Agnes* (*L'Ecole des Femmes*). She is currently Glasgow's Poet Laureate.

80   **MAGI GIBSON** lives and was educated in Glasgow, and is currently an RLF Fellow at Paisley University. Among her poetry collections are *Wild Women of a Certain Age* (2000) and *Graffiti in Red Lipstick* (2003). She also writes prose for children and young teens; and she has worked for the WEA in prisons and as a special education teacher.

81   **J. K. ANNAND** was born in Edinburgh and educated at Edinburgh University. A career in teaching spanned service in the navy. He found popularity with his bairn rhymes in Scots, particularly in *Sing it Aince with Pleasure* (1965). His adult poems, incorporating translations from Bavarian folk-song and of 'Carmina Burana', were selected in 1992.

82   **HAMISH HENDERSON** was born in Blairgowrie, and attended Dulwich College and Cambridge University. A poet, songwriter and folklorist he spent many years with the School of Scottish Studies of Edinburgh University as a field researcher, collecting traditional songs, and was a leading figure in the Scottish folk revival. Poetry includes *Elegies for the Dead in Cyrenaica* (1948) and *Collected Poems and Songs* (2000).

83   **TOM BUCHAN** was born in Glasgow. He was a teacher and lecturer, briefly at Madras University, India and subsequently in Clydebank Technical College. Besides his poetry, which included *Dolphins at Cochin* (1969) and *Poems 1969–1972* (1972), he wrote a novel and several plays. He directed festivals at Craigmillar and Dumbarton.

84   **ANON**, 'Lament of the Border Widow'. First printed in Scott's *Border Minstrelsy*, this ballad was associated by local tradition with the old tower of Henderland at the foot of Megget, near St Mary's Loch, where Scott and Hogg would commune and find inspiration.

85   **ISOBEL WYLIE HUTCHISON** was born at Carlowrie, Kirkliston. Having studied horticulture she became a botanist and collector of plants in the Arctic for the Royal Horticultural Society. Publications included *Lyrics from West Lothian* (1916) and *Lyrics from Greenland* (1935), the latter with her own water-colour sketches.

86 **DOUGLAS DUNN** was born in Inchinnan, Renfrewshire. He has published 10 poetry collections and *New Selected Poems* (2003), plus critical works, radio plays and short stories. He edited *The Faber Book of Twentieth Century Scottish Poetry* and *The Oxford Book of Scottish Short Stories*. He is newly retired from his post as a Professor of English at the University of St Andrews, having founded the post-graduate M. Litt in Creative Writing in 1993.

87 **AONGHAS MACNEACAIL** was born in Uig, Skye and lives in Carlops. He is a poet, journalist, researcher, broadcaster, script-writer and film-maker. Among his published collections in both Gaelic and English are *an seachnadh agus dàin eile/the avoiding and other poems* (1986), *Oideachadh Ceart/A Proper Schooling* (1997) and *Laoidh an Donais Oig/Hymn to a Young Demon* (2007).

88 **ALEXANDER SCOTT** was born and grew up in Aberdeen, returning to graduate there after war service. He championed Lallans and the use of Scots throughout his career as lecturer then reader in Scottish Literature at Glasgow University. His *Collected Poems* were published in 1994.

89 **GERRY CAMBRIDGE** spent many years in Ayrshire, and now lives in Bothwell, Lanarkshire. A writer and natural history pho-tographer, he founded and edits the Scottish-American poetry magazine *The Dark Horse*. His poetry collections include *'Nothing but Heather!'* (1999), *Madame Fi Fi's Farewell and Other Poems* (2003) and *Aves* (2007).

90 **VIOLET JACOB** was born at the House of Dun, near Montrose. Marrying an army officer she lived in India and the south of England, before returning and absorbing the lore and language of her native region. *Songs of Angus* (1915) enjoyed a vogue, specially in the services. She and Marion Angus share *Voices From Their Ain Countrie* (2006).

91 **EDWIN MUIR** was born in Deerness, Orkney, but when 14 moved with his family to Glasgow. In the 1920s and 30s he was with the British Council in Prague and Rome, and undertook translation work with his wife Willa. Later Warden of Newbattle Abbey College, then Visiting Professor of Poetry at Harvard, he published criticism and two volumes of autobiography. His *Complete Poems* appeared in 1991.

92 **MARY, QUEEN OF SCOTS** remains a romantic and controversial figure not least due to her suspected implication in the murder of her husband Henry Stewart, Lord Darnley and marriage to James Hepburn, Earl of Bothwell, one of the principal plotters. This is one of 12 love-sonnets in French (most likely forgeries) she was said to have written about Bothwell and produced in evidence at her trial. Translation by James Robertson (see 19)

93 **ANON**, 'Queen Mary, Queen Mary...'. A children's street game in which the participants start off standing in a line, a girl in front singing the verse, then finally form a half-circle. This wording is from James T. R. Ritchie's collection *Golden City*, first published in 1965.

94 **NORMAN MACCAIG** was born in Edinburgh, attended the Royal High School and studied classics at Edinburgh University. Following a career as a primary school teacher he tutored in Creative Writing at Edinburgh University, then at the University of Stirling. His prolific poetry output from *Riding Lights* (1955) to *Voice Over* (1988) is represented, alongside uncollected work, in *The Poems of Norman MacCaig* (2005).

95 **VALERIE GILLIES** was born in Canada, grew up in Scotland and was educated in Edinburgh and Mysore, India. She was the Edinburgh Makar from 2005 to 2008. Her poetry includes *The Chanter's Tune* (1990), *The Ringing Rock* (1995), *The Lightning Tree* (2002) and *The Spring Teller* (2008). Robertson of Crandart,

believed to have taken part in the '45, supported the tiring Prince on his march south.

96   **ANON**, 'Lassie lie near me'. This fragment, slightly varied from 'Laddie, lie near me', was added to by Robert Burns; while an extended version mentioning the Battle of Culloden concludes Hogg's *Jacobite Relics*, his 'short series of the lays of returning minstrels'.

97   **W. S. GRAHAM** was born in Greenock, trained as an engineer and studied at Newbattle Abbey College. In 1943 he moved to Cornwall, where he became a key member of the artistic scene in St Ives. Apart from two spells of teaching in New York, and regular visits abroad, he lived there for the rest of his life. *The Nightfisherman: Selected Letters* appeared in 1999, and his *New Collected Poems* in 2004.

98   **ROBERT BURNS** (v) 'John Anderson my jo, John' is a sanitised version of a bawdy song which appeared in *The Merry Muses*. In this version any hint of reproach is lost, the physical imagery simply handled, and a sense of tenderness in age touchingly conveyed.

99   **GEORGE BRUCE** was educated in his native Fraserburgh and at Aberdeen University. For three decades he was a BBC arts and features producer; and latterly a professor at several American universities. He edited and co-edited numerous anthologies of Scottish poetry, and *A Scottish Postbag*. *Today Tomorrow: Collected Poems 1933–2000* was published in 2001, and *Through the Letterbox* in 2003.

100   **ANNE MACLEOD** lives in Fortrose, in the Black Isle. She studied at Aberdeen University and is a dermatologist. Her poetry collections include *Standing by Thistles* (1997) and *Just the Caravaggio* (1999). She has also published two novels, *The Dark Ship* and *The Blue Moon Book*.

Index Of Poets

Some other books published by **LUATH** PRESS

100 Favourite Scottish Poems

Edited by Stewart Conn
ISBN 1 905222 61 0 PBK £7.99

Poems to make you laugh. Poems to make you cry. Poems to make you think. Poems to savour. Poems to read out loud. To read again, and again. Scottish poems. Old favourites. New favourites. 100 of the best.

Scotland has a long history of producing outstanding poetry. From the humblest but-and-ben to the grandest castle, the nation has a great tradition of celebration and commemoration through poetry. *100 Favourite Scottish Poems* – incorporating the top 20 best-loved poems as selected by a BBC Radio Scotland listener poll – ranges from ballads to Burns, from 'Proud Maisie' to 'The Queen of Sheba', and from 'Cuddle Doon' to 'The Jeelie Piece Song'.

Edited by Stewart Conn, poet and inaugural recipient of the Institute of Contemporary Scotland's Iain Crichton Smith Award for services to literature (2006). Published in association with the Scottish Poetry Library.

100 Favourite Scottish Poems to Read Out Loud

Edited by Gordon Jarvie
ISBN 1 906307 01 6 PBK £7.99

Poems that roll off the tongue. Poems that trip up the tongue. Poems to shout. Poems to sing. Poems to declaim. Poems that you learned at school. Poems that will stay with you forever.

Do you have a poem off by heart but always get stuck at the second verse? Can your friends and family members recite at the drop of a hat while you only have a vague memory of the poems and songs learned as a child? Or do you just want an aide-memoire to the poems you know and love? This collection includes many popular Scottish poems, from 'The Wee Cock Sparra' to 'The Four Maries', 'The Wee Kirkcudbright Centipede' to' John Anderson My Jo'; as well as poetry by Sheena Blackhall, Norman MacCaig, Jimmy Copeland, Tom Leonard and many others.

Scots have ample opportunity to let rip with old favourites on Burns Night, St Andrew's Day, or at ceilidhs and festivals. Whatever your choice, this wide-ranging selection will give you and your audience (even if it's only your mirror) hours of pleasure and enjoyment.

Luath Press Limited
committed to publishing well written books worth reading

LUATH PRESS takes its name from Robert Burns, whose little collie Luath (*Gael.*, swift or nimble) tripped up Jean Armour at a wedding and gave him the chance to speak to the woman who was to be his wife and the abiding love of his life. Burns called one of 'The Twa Dogs' Luath after Cuchullin's hunting dog in Ossian's *Fingal*. Luath Press was established in 1981 in the heart of Burns country, and is now based a few steps up the road from Burns' first lodgings on Edinburgh's Royal Mile.

Luath offers you distinctive writing with a hint of unexpected pleasures.

Most bookshops in the UK, the US, Canada, Australia, New Zealand and parts of Europe either carry our books in stock or can order them for you. To order direct from us, please send a £sterling cheque, postal order, international money order or your credit card details (number, address of cardholder and expiry date) to us at the address below. Please add post and packing as follows: UK – £1.00 per delivery address; overseas surface mail – £2.50 per delivery address; overseas air-mail – £3.50 for the first book to each delivery address, plus £1.00 for each additional book by airmail to the same address. If your order is a gift, we will happily enclose your card or message at no extra charge.

Luath Press Limited
543/2 Castlehill
The Royal Mile
Edinburgh EH1 2ND
Scotland
Telephone: 0131 225 4326 (24 hours)
Fax: 0131 225 4324
email: sales@luath.co.uk
Website: www.luath.co.uk